Rays of Hope

The Sun has been glorified and deified throughout history. When people looked up at the first light, what they saw—and what we see today—is a symbol of hope for survival in a world that is so much larger and more powerful than we.

The Sun has always had the power to chase away the nightmares that have shadowed every child's slumber and caused them to awaken in fear of the dark. Although a scientist could explain away the darkness, it often takes more than logic to comfort a little one.

Sun Lore fills the darkness with legends, lore, myths, and stories of divine light that pool into an ancient place lodged deeply within every soul. It is a celebration of the Sun worshippers of times, places, and cultures past, offered up for the insight and enjoyment of we who dwell in an age of science.

The stories of the Sun deities are legends of love, lust, power, and adventure that are sure to emblazon the soul of humankind for as long as the Sun and the horizon kiss before each twilight. *Sun Lore* is an act of worship, if n for the glory that is life.

D1430644

About the Author

Gwydion O'Hara is dedicated to the research, study, and practice of the ancient folk ways that survive today. For over twenty years, he has studied the practices of the people of the land, wherever and however they present themselves. It is this calling that has led him to write *Sun Lore* and his previous offering, *Moon Lore*.

He has traveled across the United States and Canada in the pursuit of his studies in herbology, mythology, folklore, tarot, the Pagan craft, and folk magic. Along the way, he has met, taught, and learned from many others who share his love of the old ways.

To Write to the Author

If you wish to contact the author or would like more information about this book, please write to the author in care of Llewellyn Worldwide, and we will forward your request. Both the author and publisher appreciate hearing from you and welcome your comments. Llewellyn Worldwide cannot guarantee a reply to all letters, but all will be forwarded. Please write to:

Gwydion O'Hara
c/o Llewellyn Worldwide
P.O. Box 64383, Dept. K343-3
St. Paul, MN 55164-0383, U.S.A.

Please enclose a self-addressed, stamped envelope or $1.00 to cover costs. If outside the U.S.A., enclose an international postal reply coupon.

Sun Lore

Myths and Folklore from Around the World

Gwydion O'Hara

1997
Llewellyn Publications
St. Paul, Minnesota 55164-0383, U.S.A.

FIRST EDITION
First Printing, 1997

Cover design: Tom Grewe
Cover art: Beth Wright
Interior illustrations: Robin Larsen
Editing and book design: Ken Schubert

Library of Congress Cataloging-in-Publication Data

Sun lore : myths and folklore from around the world /
  [compiled by]
  Gwydion O'Hara. -- 1st ed.
        p.   cm.
    Includes bibliographical references.
    ISBN 1-56718-343-3 (trade paper)
    1. Sun--Folklore. 2. Sun--Mythology.
    3. Sun--Religious aspects.
  I. O'Hara, Gwydion.
GR625.S86   1997   97-17276
398.26--dc21   CIP

Printed in the United States of America

Llewellyn Publications
A Division of Llewellyn Worldwide, Ltd.
P.O. Box 64383
St. Paul, MN 55164-0383, U.S.A.

To Maurice and his clan, who live and love and work by the light of the Sun, and dream upon the dawning of the Moon.

Contents

Acknowledgements xii

Introduction 1

Part 1: Origins

From the Beginning 7

From the Land of the Nile 9

The Light of Raven 12

African Twins of Light 17

The Hungry Aztec Sun 20

Quat Brings the Night 23

The Sun-Egg, Seed of All 27

The Zuni Sun-Father 30

The Sun-Baked People 33

Oloron and Great God 37

Gitche Manitou 41

The People Create the Sun 44

The River of the Sun 47

Part 2: The Solar Dignitaries

The Solar Dignitaries 51

Lords of Light 53

Sin, Who Wears the Sky 55

Agni, Triple God of Fire 60

Mithras, Lord of Harmony 63

Shamash the Just 66

Lucifer, Lord of Light. 68

Huitzilopochtli, God of Blood and Fire. 72

Ra, Father of Kings 75

Odhinn, One-Eyed Warrior 77

Vulcan, Luciferian Sun. 79

Dahzbog, Lord of Rebirth 82

Apollo, Olympian Bard 85

Lugh the Long-Handed 88

Ladies of Light 92

Hae-Sun, the Sun Maiden. 94

Yhi, Giver of Light and Life 99

Sulis' Healing Waters 104

The Mourning Sun. 106

Beiwe, Finder of the Lost 110

Walu the Dreamer 113

Amaterasu, the Rising Sun 116

Saule's Betrayal 121

Sakhmet, Goddess of Beer and Blood . 125

Hsi Wang Mu of the Setting Sun. 128

Ushas, Maid of the Dawn. 130

Bast, the Cat Goddess 132

Part 3: Other Tales

Other Tales 137

The Sun and the Bat. 139

Children of the Sun 143

Kuat Steals the Day 148

Sisters of Light. 153

Owl, Dove, and Bat 159
The Legend of Scar-Face 162
The Incestuous Light 167
Coyote's Bright Adventure 170
Rabbit Snares the Sun 175
Red Riding Sun 179
Maui's Sun Net 181
Ictinike and the Buzzard 184

Epilogue 189
Appendix A: The Solar Gods 193
Appendix B: The Solar Goddesses 195
Selected Bibliography 197

Acknowledgements

The light of the Sun embraces us all, and at times we are fortunate enough to touch each other. The love and support of friends, family, and loved ones does not go unappreciated. In addition, those at Llewellyn Publications who worked with me throughout the production of this offering, as well as that of *Moon Lore,* have been a valued inspiration. They are quickly becoming a family more than a publisher.

Introduction

There is nothing new under the Sun! One of the most dramatic realizations in undertaking a project that ties together the fibers of mythology through different times and different cultures is the inescapable fact that humanity has not changed as much as social pride would lead us to believe. In the earliest times, the Sun was regarded as a dominant force of Nature, the life-giving, life-sustaining entity by whose grace life continued to emerge victorious over seemingly insurmountable odds.

The primitive tribal peoples communicated with the simplest guttural sounds aided by a few uncertain hand signs. With childlike reasoning and understanding, they looked heavenward and saw a common uniting force—the Sun that shone on all the world without prejudice. The trees that it nurtured with its light served equally well as a home for the birds as they did as a source of nourishing fruit for the tribes. Its warmth covered all the Earth, giving equally of its comforting rays of heat. The Sun was the Father-protector and Mother-sustainer of all living creatures of the world below.

Perhaps it was this all-encompassing nature of the Sun, this protecting, nurturing goodness that gave us the first hint that this luminous orb might harbor the countenance of a divine being. This prominent, light-giving body in the heavens might certainly have embodied the essence, or at least the divine symbol, of some entity far beyond the stature of the earthbound creatures. It would only stand to reason that the unfathomable must originate with something beyond the mundane existence of mankind. Perhaps this was a hint of the great creator force itself.

So the sight of the morning Sun was welcomed at the dawn. The Sun's rising was an assurance that the God or Goddess of light and life, the creator deity, has smiled upon the puny people of the lands and allowed them to endure for another day. At the setting of the Sun, the appropriate rites were observed, the traditional rituals performed to assure that the sun would return to celebrate another dawn.

None in that faraway time would dare allude to the possibility, but here, away from the priests and priestesses who speak with the Gods and Goddesses of the Sun, we might utter the unspeakable. What if the Sun were to sink below the western horizon, and rise no more? Science and mythology agree that in eternal darkness, the world and its creatures would fade from the memory of the universe.

Sun Lore is the reconciliation of the primitive humans who lived and worshiped according to things that were beyond their understanding, and the modern men and women of reason who attempt to analyze the world in which we live. It is a celebration of the Sun worshippers of ancient times, offered up for the insight and enjoyment of their ancestors who dwell in an age of science. For it becomes clear that although scientists can explain away the darkness in ways quite foreign to our primitive predecessors, it is destined that their own children will awaken trembling, afraid of the night.

It is then that we modern, rational people will remember the old ways. Although we can talk about the revolutions of the earth about the Sun, and how it brings a constant march of day and night to the earth, it will not allay the child's fears. For emotions do not arise of reason, but from something lodged deeply within the heart, something timeless and inexplicable—the unseen, unreasoning, raw instinct that first compelled our ancestors to adore the Sun.

Part
One

Origins

From the Beginning

The Sun, in many cultures, is regarded as a creator force, the source of all life. In others, it is among the first of the beings created by a higher deity. But common to many different folklore traditions is its early appearance in the primal heavens. It is the bringer of life and of light to a newly formed world of darkness. In any case, it is one of the first players to appear as the drama of life begins to unfold upon the universal stage through the miracle of the creation.

The opening section of *Sun Lore* is a collection of tales of origin. The Sun has been there for the creatures of Earth since the beginning, and through the ages it has been ever-present, offering its nourishing light to all who dwell upon the Earth. According to many legends, the disappearance of the Sun will mark the beginning of the end of time. Should its warmth ever be withdrawn from the world, and its light fade, the universe itself will become undone.

So for as long as we know the radiance of the Sun, it is fitting that we remember the tales of its beginnings, celebrate its birth, and do honor to its sustaining golden light.

From the Land of the Nile

In the lands of the Pharaohs, the beginnings of life are recorded on ancient papyrus scrolls that narrate the workings of the god Neb-er-tcher, an early version of the Sun-god Ra. In the form of Khepera, the lord of creation, it was Neb-er-tcher who fathered all things.

Long before the rise of civilizations, there was nothing but the Sun-god and a watery abyss known as Nun. From the Sun's mouth arose all life. There were none to help the lone god in his undertaking. Neb-er-tcher found not even a solid place to stand as he began his great undertaking. From his own heart, he drew a foundation from which to conduct his great work. All the lands began to appear, and the sky above them, and the waters, stars, and all things that now make up our world and the universe around us.

As the work of creation was begun, it seemed to continue with a momentum of its own. The Sun-god would create one entity, and it in turn seemed to multiply itself and give way to an expanded creation. When at last the elements of the natural world were in place, Neb-er-tcher spit out the god Shu to hold aloft the heavens and the goddess Tefnut to bring the rains. They, in turn, gave life to the pantheon of the elder gods of the ancient Egyptians.

From his tears, Neb-er-tcher created the first men and women to inhabit the earth. The elder gods, as they grew, sent their own offspring to inhabit the earth and multiply the race of man. All things green and growing began to multiply and cover the earth. The creatures that crawl upon their bellies in the soil came into being, and moved freely about the lands.

The mighty god of light was the source of all things, and all life was of him. And as all creation proceeded and took solid form upon the Earth, the formless, self-created god of light also took on a greater definition.

That which was the essence of the Sun became an eye of the great god. The lesser light of the moon was defined in the form of his other eye. Today, when we regard the Sun throughout the day and the silver light of the moon in darkness, we can know the creator is watching carefully over the creatures of his design, as he envelops us with his light.

The Light of Raven

The Crow nation recounts a tale from the time when the earth was newborn. It was the time of the Animal People, the time of darkness before the coming of the first Grandfathers or the creation of the True People.

Raven sat in the branches of a tree and thought about the darkness that enveloped him. In time, there was a sound from out of the depths of the blackness. Raven heard the swishing of the air against a pair of wings followed by the unmistakable "Caw, caw, caw" of Old Crow.

"I'm glad you had the courtesy to call out, Old Crow," said Raven. "In this dread darkness I can not see the color of my own feathers, nor even the claws that fix me to my perch, much less the arrival of a visitor to my tree."

The two friends discussed the problem of their darkened world. They were well aware of the imminent coming of the True People to the earth, as it was foretold to them in the beginning of time. Old Crow wondered aloud what the True People might think of them upon their arrival upon the dark earth.

"They will certainly question our care of the Earth-land," said Raven. They will be bumping into trees, falling into streams, and when they turn themselves homeward, they will set their moccasins in another brave's teepee, and lie down on the skins with another brave's squaw. I'm quite certain that the True People will be not at all pleased with us."

"It is Seagull who owns the light," said Old Crow. "So many times have I asked him to open his box of light the smallest crack so that we might see where we are flying, but he keeps the light for himself and will not share it with the other Animal People."

Raven plucked a twig from his perch and began to chew. Old Crow sat in silence and waited, for he knew that it was the habit of Raven to chew twigs when he pondered matters of the most serious nature. At last, Raven let fall the twig from his beak and said, "I have thought of a plan. Seagull, who is a cousin to me, will soon shed his light upon the Earth-land. I will make him do it!"

"How are you going to convince Seagull to open his box of light?" asked Old Crow. "All of the Animal People, at one time or another, have entreated him to share the light with them, and he has been steadfast in his denial of each request. The box of light remains in his teepee for no one to see but Seagull."

"Wait and see," said Raven. "My plan will not fail." And so Old Crow did wait for Raven to enact his scheme, for Raven would not breathe a word of his idea until the deed was done.

Raven had recalled a time when he went to visit his cousin by the ocean. On his way, he flew right into some thorn bushes, and nearly tore his feathers to pieces before he could work himself free. Wanting to avoid a recurrence of this unpleasantness, Raven was careful to remember the exact location of the thorn bushes. He remembered also that Seagull always fastened his canoe to the same place—a tree along a path that led directly from Seagull's teepee. Seagull never had a problem finding the right tree when he wished to go fishing, for he would carry the box of light with him when he went. He needed only open the box a crack to be guided in the right direction.

Raven plucked some branches from the thorn bushes, and laid them upon the path that led to his cousin's canoe. When the branches were in place, Raven raced up to Seagull's teepee shouting frantically, "Your canoe has broken loose! It's being carried out to sea!"

Knowing that the tide was going out, Seagull raced from his teepee without even taking the time to put on his moccasins. He knew that if he did not act quickly his canoe would be lost to the tide. In his bare feet, Seagull ran down the trail and stepped on the thorn branches that Raven had carefully placed in the darkness. Seagull could go no further, a victim to the trap of Raven. He called out to his cousin, "Quickly! Get my canoe! Save my canoe before it is taken out to sea!"

"All right!" shouted Raven, but, of course he never moved from his place in the darkness. Raven knew that the canoe was securely fastened to the tree and in no danger of being carried off by the tide. Still, he waited for a while to keep up appearances, and then caught up with Seagull, who had made his way back to his teepee.

Seagull complained about the thorns that were lodged in his feet. Still playing the helpful cousin, Raven said that he would be pleased to pull them out, if only there was enough light to see them. In response, Seagull opened his box of light the tiniest bit. Raven pulled out a few thorns and then announced, "There are more thorns that are difficult to see. If I could have but a little more light...." Seagull, wanting to be rid of his pain, quickly obliged his cousin by opening his light box a little more. After pulling another thorn or two, Raven again asked for more light. After removing the next few, he demanded, once more, "More light!"

By the light of the increasingly more opened box, Raven removed all the thorns but one. "This last one is very difficult to get at. I shall need some more light," said Raven. As Seagull opened the box the last little bit, Raven plucked the final thorn from his feet. At the same time, he thrust out his wing, knocking the box from Seagull's hold. When the box fell to the hard ground, it shattered in pieces, and the light of the world was no longer contained.

Thus, say the legends, was the Sun born and the darkness lifted from the Earth-lands.

African Twins of Light

*I*n some cultures, it is impossible to divorce or even distinguish the sky deities of Moon and Sun from one another. They are almost considered as a single being. Such is the case in the legends of the Fon people, who were the twelfth-century ancestors of the modern-day people now who inhabit the African nation we call Dahomey.

The actual creator of the world was the Great Mother, known to the Fon people as Nana Buluku. After the creation of the world, Nana Buluku bore the Sun and Moon, twins who came to be known as Mawu and Lisa. The creation of the world was no small task, and after the birth of her children, Nana Buluku retired from the scene and left the rest of the work of the creation to the divine twins.

Mawu was the Moon. She ruled the night and made her home in the western sky. Lisa was the Sun. He reigned over the day, and made his dwelling in the east. In the early times, they were all that existed. They went about their own ways, separated by sky.

In time, however, there was an eclipse. There, in the the darkened sky, perhaps they noticed each other in a different way than they ever had previously. Or perhaps they just relinquished themselves to the shadows, and acted as all men and women might in the embrace of the night. It is in this moment that Mawu and Lisa became the Mother and Father of creation.

Together, they gave life to fourteen gods—seven sets of divine twins. And with the births of their children, the gods of light became as one. They were no longer to be known as Mawu and Lisa, Sun and Moon. They became Mawu-Lisa, the divine union of creation, the Light.

Mawu-Lisa, one day, beckoned to all of the divine children. To each set of twins, a rulership was given. The first was given the rulership of the Earth. The second remained in the sky, charged with command over Thunder and Lightning. Next the rulership of Iron was passed down. It was the charge of the Iron gods to clear the jungles to make way for human habitation, and to pass on to the people their tools and weapons to ensure their survival.

Other twins were appointed the rulership of the waters of the earth, and the fishes and sea creatures that inhabit them. The rulership of the birds and creatures of the lands were allotted to others. The care of trees and growing things was assigned, as was jurisdiction over death.

In passing on the responsibility of the creation to the divine twins, Mawu-Lisa took steps to ensure that the lesser gods were never seen by mankind. That is why tribal lore still tells of the Spirit of the Earth, the Spirit of Sky, the Spirit of Iron, the Spirit of Thunder and Lightning. No human eyes have ever set upon the gods who rule over the kingdoms of the creation. But the wise tribesman know well that it is the greater gods of light who are truly responsible for their world. They recall the legends each night as they sleep beneath the protective eye of the silver light of the night, and each day as they rise to meet the Sun they hail Mawu-Lisa, their creator.

The Hungry Aztec Sun

*I*n trying to understand the miracles of the universe, many people relate the divine world to their own. They see gods and goddesses as men and women who dwell upon a loftier plane, but who have the same feelings and thoughts as their earthbound creations, and know the same desires, dreams, and needs.

This is evident in the Sun tales of the Aztec people. Like all creatures, the Sun was considered to be dependent upon food and water for nourishment.

And for want of the means to sustain life, many Suns have faded from the sky.

The first Sun was known as Atonatiuh, the Water-Sun. It had its only nourishment in the water absorbed over centuries of time from the lands of the earth. However, this was not sufficient to sustain the life of the Sun. In time, it became fairly consumed by the liquid it took for its nourishment, and developed into little but a great ball of floating water. Unable to sustain its light, and unable to hold its bloated mass of water, Atonatiuh exploded upon the earth, creating the oceans and rivers of the world, but also bringing complete destruction to the plant and animal life that inhabited the land.

Following the demise of the Water-Sun, other Suns were created. Many failed, again for lack of sustenance. Finally, a solution was found that led not only to the birth of the Sun that we now see riding above the day, but brought about the creation of humankind in the bargain.

Xolotl, the Aztec God of the Evening Star, is believed to be the designer of the plan. Through offering the greatest sacrifice, by tearing out his own heart, Xolotl gave the newborn Sun the strength to ascend to its place in the sky. In this way, he also created the human race to be a source of nourishment to the newly formed luminary—to fight and slay each other so that the Sun might be nourished by their flesh.

The Aztecs believe that Xotl's design explains the jurisdiction of the Sun over our fate, and that our wars and strife must continue for the sake of the Sun's sustenance. This plan seems without compassion, even to the point of being cruel in its enactment. Yet the ways of gods are strange, and often beyond the reach of human understanding. Certainly, there must be a wisdom that escapes us in this design, for the Sun still rises each day, and people still fight each other; so apparently the Sun's survival is assured for some time to come.

Quat Brings the Night

Often in creation mythology, the Sun is the first entity to appear in a void universe. This is true in the cosmology of the Melanesian natives of the Banks Islands, as in many other cultures.

In the beginning, there was only light. Beneath the light was a stone. This was Quatgoro, the divine Mother. The stone split in half, and the twelve gods of Melanesian legend were born.

The firstborn was Quat. He is remembered in legends as a great hero, a demi-god, and even as the Sun God of the Banks Islands. His adventures are many, but this is a tale of Quat's role in the creation, and in the coming of night.

As soon as he emerged from the stone, Quat began thinking about creating things. He set about making stones, trees and other plants, and pigs. He fashioned the first human from a tree he had made. First, he carved the arms and legs. Then he carefully cut in delicate hands and feet, fingers and toes. He made the torso from another piece of the tree, and eyes and ears and lips from yet another fragment. When each individual piece had been carved, Quat fitted them together to make the wooden figure complete.

After completing six of these wooden figures, Quat lined them in a row in front of him, then took hold of his sacred drum and began to play. With each drumbeat, the wooden figures became more animated. They began to move, very stiffly at first, still bound by the unyielding wood of which they were fashioned. As Quat played on, however, the wooden people became more fluid in their movements.

Quat played faster and faster. As he did, the human figures broke free from the nature of their wooden beginnings. They were able to move freely, to walk, to run, and to dance.

This was the beginning of the human race. By design, Quat created three men and three women so each man and woman would pair as husband and wife. Through Quat's cleverness and the magic of the sacred drum, humankind came to be.

It was the plan of Quat that men and women should live forever. Had it not been for his meddling brother, it would be as Quat designed. But his brother was called Tangaro the Fool, and was true to his name.

Tangaro watched the creation of Quat and decided to follow in his way. After carving the figures from a tree, Tangaro played the magic drum and watched them begin to move. But after a time, he tired of this game. He dug a hole and placed his carved figures in it for safekeeping. Then he covered it up with dirt.

Tangaro was easily distracted by a great many things. It was not until a week later that he remembered his wooden carvings and returned to dig them up.

When he unearthed his work, he found that the wood had rotted beneath the soil. His figures smelled so foul that he was forced to return them to the hole and cover them back up. This was the beginning of death in the world—all because of the whims of a fool.

In time, the twelve brothers complained about the constant light in the world. At the insistence of his brothers, Quat began thinking about creating something to arrest the brightness. He remembered hearing about a place on the far edge of the sky that was without light, so he climbed aboard his canoe and set sail. It seemed he would sail on forever, but at last he reached his destination. He found himself in a place where there was only darkness. He was told that the name of this place was Night.

Quat took a piece of Night to carry home with him. On his journey homeward, he came upon a group of islands. The people of the islands traded him one of his pigs for some creatures of air that were like nothing that Quat had ever seen.

When he reached home, Quat brought out his treasures. With the gift of Night, the world, at last, had some relief from constant brightness. And the birds heralded the return of the Sun when the time of Night was ended.

This is how it has been since that time. We now take our rest from labor when the world retreats from light, and when the birds announce the return of day, we renew our tasks. But it took a Sun God to give us rest from the light.

The Sun-Egg, Seed of All

The mythology of India is rich with tales of transition. We see changing faces of the Hindu deities as the universe undergoes the great metamorphosis that was the beginning of the world—the Creation. According to the legends of the land, all life came from the Sun.

It is said that in the beginning, there was nothingness. There was no land, no life—naught but an endless sea of dark waters. Upon the waters floated a lotus blossom. It was from this sacred blossom that the first signs of life appeared.

From deep within the lotus blossom rose an egg. It was golden in color, with the bright splendor of the Sun. It ascended above the soft petals of the blossom, and was plunged into the midst of the dark primordial sea. It was from a lust for existence, a passion for life, that the Sun-egg came into being. At first, this fevered passion manifested as fire. As the fever grew, the fire fanned out into rays. These golden rays condensed into a cloud, and from this glowing cloud the world's oceans were formed.

Next to emerge from the Sun-egg was Brahma Prajapati, the Father of All. Looking around, he saw nothing but water. He held the great passion that caused his birth, but was devoid of wisdom or understanding. He questioned his purpose, alone in these endless waters. In his great confusion, Prajapati fell to tears. The tears that fell into the water became the earth. Some that he wiped away became the air that enveloped the land. There were others that he wiped upwards. These became the heavens above the earth.

It was then that Prajapati created the Asuras, the demons, as well as the darkness. From the substance of his own body, he then created men and women, and moonlight also emerged. He created the seasons and twilight, and then the gods, and day.

To sustain his creations, Prajapati fed the Asuras milk from an earthenware bowl. The men and women of the earth were given milk in a dish of wood. The seasons drank the milk of creation from a bowl of fine silver. The gods, in a bowl of gold, with the brightness of the Sun itself, were sustained by the sacred Soma, the nectar of life.

As the Sun rises to fullness each day, the universe recounts the tale of the creation. The first rays of dawn are like the first flames of passion that emerge from the Sun-egg. The morning dew is like the clouds that formed the first waters. At midday, the Sun is in its fullest glory. This is when the creatures of the earth thrive, reflecting the moment of their own creation. The setting of the Sun, as the last golden rays peek over the horizon, is the time of the creation of the gods, who reflect the light of Prajapati in the moonlight.

Lastly, the Sun disappears below the Western horizon, and the world is plunged into darkness. This is a reflection of the final creation of Prajapati, which was the devourer of life—the creature called Death.

So it began, and has continued since that time. Each day, we can look at the progression of the Sun across the sky, and remember the tales of our beginnings. As we do, we are also made aware that the divine hand that gave life also created the instrument of its loss. And all of this proceeded from the golden splendor that was the Sun-egg, seed of creation.

The Zuni Sun-Father

From New Mexico come the legends of Awonawilona, the Creator-god of the Zuni people. As with many stories of creation, the tale begins in a time before time, in a world of absolute darkness.

Nothing knew existence but Awonawilona, who was alone in the endless night. Eventually, the Creator conceived the idea of light. He gave this idea so much attention that he became his thought, and swelled from the depths of his being outward as a mist. The mist of light floated upwards and was transformed. The cloud that was the All-Father became the Sun, and the surrounding darkness was penetrated by his brightness.

Still, the mist that surrounded Awonawilona thickened. From it came the waters, and the Sun-Father rested upon the waters of his creation. From out of his own being, Awonawilona created the substance that formed Earth-Mother and Sky-Father. Earth-Mother created the lands in which the Zuni tribes would make their dwellings. She created the snow that stays upon the mountain peaks that rise high into the heavens. Sky-Father created the rain. Earth-Mother caught the rain mists in hollows of her lands to form the lakes and rivers.

From grains within his hand, Sky-Father created the stars that would guide the earth children in the darkness of night. At the same time, he buried some grain beneath the soil to be nourished into fine golden corn by his rains.

At last, the earth children themselves were created. They were formed within a cave in the newly created Earth, and were a long time in their formation. The Sun-Father sent two mighty beings to oversee the development of the earth children. These were the Twin Brothers of Light. To them, he gave his own great wisdom to ensure the success of their mission.

The Twin Brothers found the cave in which the earth people had begun to form. Within the cave were growing things—plants, grasses, and vines. The brothers breathed upon the stems of the growing greenery, making them grow faster and stronger. These vines and grasses twisted together to make a ladder that led to a second cave.

The men and women and other creatures of the earth ascended the ladder. From there, they were led to a third cave, and finally a fourth. As they came to each new level, the Twin Brothers taught them a higher wisdom. At the first, they learned the basic instincts of survival. In the second cave, the creatures learned to see beyond themselves and think to the future. Here they began to multiply in number, and to think beyond their own existence to the survival of their races.

In the third cave, the earth people again increased in number. This cave was full of light, bringing the beginnings of knowledge to the creatures of earth. The fourth cave was even brighter than the third. Here were the beginnings of truth and perception, the beginning of seeking. The Twin Brothers taught the earth creatures about the Sun-Father, and to always seek his light.

From the fourth cave, the newly created creatures were led to the fifth and final cave of their journey, which held the beginnings of understanding. It was from here that the Mighty Ones led them into the upper world where they were to live and love under the light of the Sun-Father.

The Sun-Baked People

Though many cultures look to the Sun as the beginning of all creation, in some legends creation was not a lone accomplishment. A major undertaking, it required the efforts of more than one artisan before it was complete. The Crow people tell such a legend of the creation.

As it is remembered, the Great Spirit descended from Sky-land to begin the work of bringing the first people to the land. The Great One made a hole in the sky. Through it, he pushed massive white clouds, piling them high, one upon the other. He amassed so many clouds that they most nearly touched the earth from that hole in the sky. When this was done, the Great One climbed down the clouds in two great giant steps, and walked upon the earth.

From the place where he set foot upon the soil, the Great Spirit headed south. He knew the Sun favored the lands to the south, and the Great One sought the Sun's help in bringing the first people into the world.

The Great One sat beside a large pile of clay on the southern plain. He took a portion in his great hand and began to work it into shape. He rolled it, kneaded it, and shaped it with his strong fingers. When he was done, he had made the form of a man. Gently, he laid the newly formed image on the ground and covered it with leaves.

It was then that the Great One addressed the Sun who had been watching his work from some distance. "Sun," he said, "Go sit in the tree that stands nearby, and bake this newly formed creature with your heat." The Sun climbed the maple tree pointed out by the Great One, and began to carry out his instructions. Not wanting to disappoint the Great Spirit, the Sun devoutly tended his duty while the Great One rested from his toil.

After a time, the Great One awoke from his rest and went to retrieve the clay figure the Sun had so diligently baked. When the covering of leaves was removed, he saw that the figure was burned black.

"This is not exactly what I had in mind," said the Great One to the Sun. The black man was sent away, and instructed not to return to this land for some time. Then the Great Spirit set about to try his work again. He fashioned another figure of clay, and covered it with leaves as he had done before. This time, however, he sent the Sun to sit on a far-off mountain, and cautioned him to use his heat sparingly in baking the clay figure.

The Great One settled down for a nap as he had before, and left the Sun to finish the work of creating the first person. This time, the Sun was very careful not to cast too much heat upon the clay figure, so that it would not bake as dark as the first one.

When the Great One awoke and the figure was uncovered, it was not blackened as the first had been. In fact, at seeing the results of the second baking, the Great One exclaimed, "Why, Sun, this figure is hardly cooked at all!" So he sent this new white man off to other lands, telling him not to return for a long, long time.

The Great One fashioned another figure from the clay, and covered it with leaves like before. This time he had the Sun sit in the nearby maple tree, but send his heat in another direction. In this way, thought the Great Spirit, the figure will be heated only indirectly by the Sun, and should be baked to perfection.

When the leaves were removed from this latest figure, it was a red man that was uncovered. The

Great One was pleased with this latest creation, and made many more in the same manner. Women and children were also formed from the clay and baked by the Sun until they were red. This was the creation of the first real tribe upon the earth.

The Great One never spoke of the black man and the white man that were previously made from the clay. It was not until many years later that the Crow people learned of their existence when they came from their far places to the lands where the tribes dwelt. That there could be people upon the earth other than those like themselves was a shock to the Crow. Yet, according to the legends, it was their own Great Spirit who fashioned these beings of black and white, and baked them under their own hot Sun.

Oloron and Great God

There are cultures that make little distinction between sky and sun. The Yoruba tribe of Nigeria is among these. Their greatest god, their Creator, is Oloron. He owns the sky and the sun, and is, in fact, the essence of both.

In the beginning, there was no solid earth anywhere. The world was a watery place. The only semblance of dry land was the marshy areas, which were more water than earth. There could be no people to inhabit the earth until there was a solid place for them to stand. Oloron realized this, and began making plans to solidify some of the watery wasteland below so that the creation of humanity could begin.

Oloron summoned one of the other divine spirits to help in the work ahead. This was the one called "Great God." Oloron gave Great God a shell containing a small bit of earth. Also within the shell were a pigeon cock and hen. He was instructed to take the shell and to make solid land in the world below.

Great God went down to the marshlands. He spilled out the earth from the shell and set the pigeons upon it. They scratched at the earth from the shell with their feet until the marshland was covered with it. This was how the watery waste that was once the earth became firm and solid.

Oloron named this new land *Ife*, which means wide, for it was determined that this new creation was indeed wide enough for the work that lay ahead. Upon the firm land of Ife, Oloron placed a house. It is said that all other houses were born of this first one placed there by the hand of Oloron.

Then it was time for the next stage of preparation to begin. Again, Oloron summoned Great God to help him. Great God was instructed to descend once more to Ife and to plant trees that would be the food for the race of men and women when their time came. Great groves of trees were planted. There were nuts and fruits for the people to eat. They would drink the juices of the newly planted trees. Rain was sent from the sky world to nourish the trees and make them grow. Great God planted more and more trees so that food would be plentiful for this new race.

At last, all was in readiness for the people that would inhabit the earth below. Oloron set Great God to form the human figures from bits of earth. He formed the heads and the bodies of these images, and brought the figures to Oloron to give them life.

Great God did not know how to give his figures life, and was jealous of Oloron for his ability to animate them. In order to discover how this was done, Great God hid among his newly sculpted images and watched as Oloron sat down to bring them to life. But Oloron is an all-knowing god. He was aware of Great God's jealousy, and of his plan to discover the secret of life. To prevent him from seeing his work, Oloron put Great God into a deep sleep. By the time the would-be watcher awoke, the human figures were filled with life. Great God never saw what magic of Oloron's brought this miracle about.

So it is that Great God is charged with the duty of forming the bodies of people, but only Oloron can grant them life. Great God has never quite gotten over his foiled attempt to learn the secret of bestowing life. Sometimes when he fashions the figures that are to become the people of the earth world, his dissatisfaction shows through. He might mar their figures, or make them deformed, ugly, or incomplete. But he is usually diligent in his work, and is also responsible for children with bodies of grace and beauty, and faces that are wondrous to behold.

We must look to Great God as the benefactor of our physical virtues. But for our life itself, we honor only Oloron, essence of the Sun and Sky.

Gitche Manitou

The gods of some peoples are more familiar, more approachable, than they appear in other cultures. This is true of the multi-faceted "Great Spirit" of the Arapaho nations of the eastern United States. These tribes know their highest god spirit by the name *Gitche Manitou*. He is all that was there at the advent of time, and he is the great Creator.

Like the supreme deity of many American tribal peoples, Gitche Manitou manifests as the Sun. In the time before the creation of the Arapaho people, Gitche Manitou wandered alone in a watery world. As he wandered, he looked for a place where the firm earth would be made to rise above the waters.

The Great Spirit called together all the water creatures to help him with the work of creating the dry lands that would come to be the world of the Arapaho. He sent out a call to all the water snakes, the turtles, and other reptiles. He also summoned all the water birds to help in the great work that he was about to undertake.

For their part, the turtles knew where to find earthy clay far beneath the water. They retrieved the clay from the depths of the watery world and passed it up to the water birds. The birds brought the clay in their beaks, laying it before Gitche Manitou. Thousands of them made their way to the Great Spirit until enough clay had been collected for the creation to begin.

Gitche Manitou dried the clay over his sacred pipe. He made the dry land by carefully shaping and molding the wet clay that the water creatures had brought. When the work was done, he admired his artistry. This would certainly be a fitting world for the Arapaho people.

The human race was next to be created. As with the earth lands, Gitche Manitou carefully and diligently shaped the tiny bodies of the human forms from clay. When a form was properly shaped and dried over the sacred pipe, the Great Spirit breathed life into the clay, and the first humans came to be.

Gitche Manitou continued at his work for some time, until he had enough clay figures to begin the human race. He fashioned some men, women, and perhaps a few children. It was a proud accomplishment, and Gitche Manitou was pleased with the results. Even the emergence of Bitter Man from his clay dolls did not lessen the pleasure of his accomplishment.

Bitter Man was the embodiment of human frailty that was created along with the other firm, healthy figures from the clay. He was old age and infirmity. He was death. Still, Great Spirit worked happily until his undertaking was complete.

It is by his error in creating Bitter Man that we realize the fallibility, the "humanness" of Gitche Manitou. He is Master of Light, Creator of the World, Giver of Life, but also very much like those he created, and very approachable. This is why the Arapaho people know Gitche Manitou, the Great Spirit, also as the "Ancestor with the Sacred Pipe."

The People Create the Sun

In many legends the Sun is the great benefactor, the supreme creative force. However, among the Luiseno people of the far southwestern United States, it is the Sun who is beholden to us. The Sun did not always exist, and perhaps would not now, but for the efforts of humanity.

To the Luiseno, it was Mother Earth and Father Sky who created the world. They came together to form the earth and the heavens, the plants and animals that lived upon the soil, the creatures of the air and the water, and, of course, the First People.

The world that was left for the First People by the Mother and Father was a dark world. With no light to illuminate their way, the First People wandered aimlessly and blindly through their world, continually tripping, bumping into each other, and falling down.

Exactly who it was has been obscured by time, but one of the First People conceived of the idea of a Sun to dispel the Earth's endless night. This was easily done, for the First People were gifted with superior craftsmanship. Once the work was done, however, it was discovered that there were some flaws in the original design.

Resting upon the earth, the heat of the newly-born Sun was far too intense for people to withstand. And its light, though adequately bright, was too close to the land to be seen above the trees and the hills. The Sun creator determined that the proper place for his creation was in the sky. This would lessen the intense heat to a bearable level, and offer a position where every corner of the earth could benefit from the light.

The wise artisan set right to work in constructing a net woven of milkweed. Then he called on all of the First People to convene at the site of his new creation. Together, they spread out the net upon the ground, and placed the Sun at its center. Each taking hold of an edge of the great milkweed net, they began to bounce the Sun up and down. With a final thrust, they threw the Sun soaring high into the sky.

Up and up the Sun flew, up to the northern heavens. But the First People were not pleased with this placement. They retrieved the Sun and tried again. This time, they were careful to pull away from the north when they bounced the Sun in their net. Unfortunately, they were overly cautious in their attempt not to repeat the same mistake, for the Sun flew off to the south this time.

The third attempt to situate the Sun in the heavens sent it upward in a westerly direction, then plummeting back down to the net. One last try found the Sun settling in the eastern sky. All the First People agreed that this was the proper place for the Sun.

Finally, with the Sun in the east as it should be, the First People raised their voices in chants and song. The magic of their chorus set the Sun in an annual course that would bring it sometimes closer to the north, sometimes closer to the southern lands, depending on the season.

The Luiseno people say that this is how the journey of the Sun began, and perhaps there is some truth in the legend. After all, the Sun still begins the day from its home in the eastern sky, and as we progress through the seasons, we find the Sun sometimes favors the northern sky, sometimes the south. So has it always been since the First People created the Sun.

The River of the Sun

The Desana tribe of southeastern Columbia are in agreement with many other cultures in regard to the Creator Sun. They revere the Sun as the divine designer of the universe, and the force behind all that exists in the worlds of substance and spirit. Like other peoples, they honor the Creator Sun as the earth is warmed throughout the day by his golden, life-giving light. However, the Desana also see the evidence of their creator god throughout the night, as they look up at the starry skies.

According to the legend, the first thing the Sun made was the Milky Way, but it is not a mass of stars—it is the river of the Sun. Its turbulent currents carry bundles of palm that are tossed with the rolling of its waves, and it is these yellowish white palm bundles that give the Sun's river its color. In the body of the palm leaves is carried the essence of the entire universe.

All disease, pestilence, waste, and suffering rises from the dark underworld beneath the western horizon, and floats into the sky on the river of the Sun. All the goodness and light of Creator Sun is carried in the waters of the Milky Way as well. When a Desana hunter kills his prey and feeds it to the tribe, he is drawing from the great spiritual goodness of the river of the Sun. When a tribal shaman wishes to enter into a spiritual endeavor, whether for healing, prayer, or magic, he reaches to the sky to feel the power of the Sun river that stretches across the sky.

The Desana legend serves to keep the tribal people always mindful that they owe their existence, all they have, and all that they are to the Creator Sun. The lesson of the legend is made manifest each day as they regard the brilliance of the golden Sun. And by night, they see evidence of the great creator in the River of the Sun.

Part
Two

The Solar
Dignitaries

The Solar Dignitaries

*A*s Creator, Bringer of Life, Messenger of Death, the great benefactor or the great destroyer of the race of mankind, the Sun has been glorified and deified throughout history. When the people looked up at first light, they were greeted by the brightness of the new day. What they saw then, and what many see today, was not merely the inexplicable wonder of Nature that gave hope for their survival in a world so much larger and powerful than they. They saw the symbol or the essence of their God or Goddess.

Through changing times, and through cultures that rise and fade away through the centuries, the Sun has been ever-present. From its place in the heavens, it has received the praise and reverence of countless generations of the earth inhabitants below, and has been known by many names.

It has been said that it is impossible for the eyes of a mortal to look directly into the face of the divine. Perhaps the ancient civilizations who worshiped the Sun knew this, and realizing that they could not sustain a gaze into the fiery Sun for but an instant, knew that the light of day was of the divine realm.

Though the designers of the old solar religions of the world have passed away, their memories survive in their legends about their solar Gods and Goddesses. There are few who remember to greet the Sun with the reverence of old, with the awe-inspired love that was once the way of all people. Yet there are still those who glory in the warm rays of the deity, who see the fire of warmth through the snows of winter, and the glory of light in the dark of night. For these bright souls, the tales of the solar dignitaries have special meaning. And for all humanity, the stories of the Sun deities are legends of love, power, and adventure. Their presentation here is, in itself, an act of worship—if not for the gods of old, then for the beauty and glory that is Life.

Lords of Light

Generally, the solar deity is seen as male creator-god. He is often the husband of the moon and sire of the stars. There are many legends of the Sun God that describe his birth in the east, his rise to full stature at midday, and the waning of his reign at sunset. At times, these tales tell of the daily rise and fall due to some outside agent. Other times, they are narratives of birth, growth, death, and reincarnation

The solar deity may be a god of many aspects. Depending on the culture, he may be the messenger of peace, the essence of eternal wisdom, and/or the caretaker of the mortal races of both human and animal kind. As a warrior god, the Lord of the Sun might lead tribes into victory against their enemies, or he may demand blood sacrifice to assure the people's success in war.

In some cases, he may present a picture of conflicting aspects. He can be seen bestowing life with one hand and taking it away with the other. The Sun God is Father, Brother, Lover, Friend. He is always stable, yet always changing as the thoughts and needs of his people change.

The solar divinity is known by many symbols in different cultures. His is the Sun-disk, the wheel, the spider in the center of his web. His is the eagle, the falcon, the dove, and the hawk. His is the lion, the ram, the bull, and the dragon.

The Sun God is a vision of honor, of strength, and of courage. He is a defender as well as a dealer of justice. His character is often the product of the culture that worships him. Yet even as they are responsible for their view of the Sun, their dependence on and reverence for the deity is unreserved. Just as the Sun as it filters through the clouds yields a myriad of colors, so there are innumerable facets to the God of the Sun. These stories present some of them.

Sin, Who Wears the Sky

Many Native American cultures revere a sky deity. In the lore of British Columbian tribes, this deity takes on an unusual character. Sin, the Sky God of the Haida tribe, is portrayed as the essence of the Sun, yet the incidental actions of this divine child also make him the designer of the appearance of the sky. This is his story as the Haida tell it.

One of the Haida chiefs had a daughter, a beautiful maid at the threshold of womanhood. One day, she decided to journey down to the beach to spend the day digging in the sand. After she had been at her task for some time, the maiden uncovered a cockle-shell.

The young woman delighted in her first find of the day, but hoping for greater treasure, decided to continue her digging. As she was about to cast the shell away, she heard the sound of a baby crying. Examining the cockle-shell more closely, she was astonished to find the form of a small baby inside.

It was then that the maiden stepped over the invisible line that separates the child from the woman, as feelings of motherly love and protective nurturing swelled up within her. She tenderly wrapped the child in a warm cover and carried it home, holding it close to her breast. She named the child Sin, and it was through the depth of her love and care that the child quickly grew to be strong and healthy. He soon began to stand and walk, then to run and play.

Mother and child were sitting together one afternoon when the child began making movements with his hands as if he was drawing back the string of an imaginary bow. Seeing this, the woman took a copper bracelet from her wrist and fashioned it into a bow, just the right size for his small hands. She strung the copper bow and gave it to the child with a couple of small arrows that she made. The little brave was pleased with his mother's gift, and wasted no time in making use of it for hunting. Every day, he returned to his mother's side with the prize of his labors. One day he brought home a goose, and at another time a woodpecker was felled by his tiny weapon.

Up until this point, Sin's life was inseparable from his mother's. All of their days were spent in each other's company. However, when Sin began to journey out on his hunting adventures, his mother did not spend her days alone awaiting the return of her beloved son. Unknown to the young Sun God, a carpenter had befriended his mother. They spent their days together while the child was on the hunt.

It was not until a later time that Sin was surprised by the involvement of the carpenter in his mother's life. One day, after a fruitful but exhausting hunt, Sin returned to his mother's side, and they settled down to rest from the day's labors. When Sin awoke, he found himself in a fine new dwelling. It was finely carved and rich in color: bright reds, blues, greens, and yellows.

The carpenter married Sin's mother. He was a good husband to her, and a kind father to Sin. Sin learned many things from his new father, and the carpenter learned from his son.

There came a day when the carpenter took the boy out to the seashore and had him look out over the wide ocean. As long as the youth did this, the weather remained fair. Another time, the two went out fishing together. Sin gave his father some sacred words to speak. When the carpenter did this, there was a violent pull on their fishing line and their canoe was dragged three times around their island home. When the turbulent struggle stopped, they hauled in their line. On it was a great sea monster covered with fresh halibut for their evening meal.

In time, Sin grew to manhood. His father painted his face with golden color, and the brave journeyed out wearing a garment of wren feathers. His mother watched him as he rose above her and ascended high above the ocean. Then Sin changed his garment to one made of the bright feathers of the blue jay. Again he rose above the ocean, and shone in blue-gold splendor. One more time, the youth changed garments. This time, he wore the feathers of the woodpecker. When he rose above the ocean, the waves reflected the deep red of the woodpecker's crest, as if the waters were covered in fire.

When he finally descended to the side of his mother, Sin said, "Beloved Mother, I am now a man. I can abide with you no longer." And as he took his leave, Sin made her a gift of magic so that they would never truly be apart.

Because of this gift, Sin's mother is now known as Fair Weather Woman, and she dwells in the winds. When the sea air turns cold, she makes offerings of feathers to her son. The feathers are flakes of white snow, and remind the golden child that the people long to see the splendor of his shining countenance once more.

The people of the Haida tribe still watch for Sin to rise in the sky. When he soars above the ocean wearing the feathers of the wren, they see the first light of day. The bright blue of the jay is the sky at midday, and when the waves reflect the red fire of the woodpecker, it is the end of day. When the winds turn icy, and Fair Weather Woman covers the land with snow, they long for the golden splendor of Sin once more, for it is by his presence that the earth will be warmed by golden light, and the fishing will be good.

Agni, Triple God of Fire

Reminiscent of the many lunar goddesses who represent the moon in the three different aspects of crescent, full, and dark, is the Hindu fire god Agni. His aspects do not include morning, midday, and setting sun as one may expect. Agni is the god of lightning, of the domestic fire used by humans, and of solar fire.

Agni is pictured with two faces—both red, the color of fire. These represent earth-fire, the controlled fire used to clear areas of forest land to build their cities, and Sun-fire, the blazing fire of the Sun. He has three legs. These represent three vital phases in the lives of humans. They are the sacrificial fire, the marriage fire, and the funeral fire. Agni has seven arms: one to reach out to each of the seven continents of the world, and seven tongues of flame emit from his open mouth.

At the Hindu marriage rites, the newly united couple walks seven times around the wedding fire to procure Agni's blessing. His aid is enlisted by lovers for the fire of passion that fulfills their coupling. His is the hot fire of love and sexual union.

In every household, Agni has a prominent place. He is the master of the wild blazing fire of the Sun, but he is also the god of the hearth. Every hearth fire is his place of worship, and his eyes can see through every flame. Through his place in the hearth, he knows and sees all that transpires in every home.

Hindus consider fire to be the great cleanser. It has the power to burn away all that is unclean, and to purge all the sins and misdeeds of the world. It is for this reason that the bodies of the dead are burned. It is the great cleansing that prepares the soul for its continued journey.

There is a legend told of the time when Agni learned a lesson in moderation. Being a sacred figure in many households, there was never a shortage of offerings made to the Sun God. At one time, he became overzealous in his consumption of these sacrifices. Greedily, he consumed all that was offered.

Just as might happen to a man or woman that overindulges in food or drink, Agni could not escape the results of his gluttony. He needed to recover from his divine "morning after." In the end, he only was able to restore himself by returning some fire to the earth. He burned down the forest lands of Khandava, and so relieved his bloat of fire.

On this occasion, Agni also became known as the god of destructive fire. He is not restricted in his scope. He is a god of devastation as well as of benevolence. He is the roaring blaze of the fires of disaster as well as the comforting of the hearth-fire and the warming fires of the Sun.

Mithras, Lord of Harmony

*T*here are many deities that adapt to the needs of their worshippers, not as simply as changing a doctrine of a sacred trust, but actually transforming their essence. This is true of the Sun God Mithras. He has survived the march of time as well as the dominance of one culture over another. The secret of his survival was the ability to adapt to the needs of the populace.

Originating in the pantheon of Hindu India, where he was known as Mitra, this Sun God was the brother of Varuna, God of the Moon.

Together, the twin lights maintained order in the universe, and brought a life of peace to humankind. Mitra was responsible for friendship and honesty, while Varuna took charge of the fulfillment of promises.

As times began to change, so did the essence of Mitra, and even the meaning of his name. Originally, Mitra was a sky deity. His name meant "sun" or "sky." As he was brought into closer contact with the needs of his people, his name came to mean "world." Drawing still closer to the world of mortals, the name Mitra meant "community" or "village." Finally, as time progressed, it meant "friend."

Perhaps it was this humanizing of the divinity that led to his loss of popularity in India. However, when he was no longer highly revered in the land of his origin, he migrated to neighboring Persia. There, he rose to prominence once more as Mithra, God of the Dawn.

As a Persian god, Mithra still embraced the ideals of peace. Under his influence, deadly enemies could sit down together to share a meal and sort out their differences. Together, they would observe the proper rites and honor Mithra with the sacrifice of a bull.

In Persia, Mithra developed yet another side to his character. While he was still a god of peace, he also became a god of justice. He not only encouraged friendship, honor, and right action, but began to punish those who violated his principles of peace. He despised the liar, the vow-breaker, and the insincere.

Later, in order to bring harmony to the world, Mithra became a savior as the dying god—the great bull of the Sun who sacrificed himself so that all the world might know peace.

In Rome, the Sun bull was reincarnated as Mithras. As in Persia, his rites included the sacrifice of a bull. This sacrifice was believed to grant his favor, assuring his followers peace, prosperity, and fertility.

The mystery cult of Mithras survived even after the rise of Christianity. One of the promises of Mithras was the survival of the soul after physical death. This granted his followers a guarantee of immortality. Those who lived their lives under threat of death found this particularly desirable. Among the warrior classes, specifically the Roman soldiers, his worship continued for centuries after the birth of Jesus and the Christian church.

Always with a benevolent side, yet strangely popular among men of war, Mithras is remembered in peace as well as war. He is honored for the hand of peace and friendship that binds the families into a community, as well as by those who live by conflict. Mithras takes his place as lord of both.

Shamash the Just

The Sun God of the ancient Babylonians was Shamash. He is unique among the Solar deities in that he is the essence of the principles of right and justice. In fact, he and his wife Aya had two children who were to carry on the work of the Sun deity. Their names were Misharu, which means "law," and Kittsu, which translates as "justice." It is said that the light of Shamash is such that no wrongdoer can escape his sight. The rays of light he casts down from the Sun act as a net to entrap criminals. It was also

Shamash that delivered the famous Code of Hammurabi to the legendary king. This was one of the first systems of law and justice known in the world of men.

Unique, also, is the vision of the arrival of Shamash at the beginning of his journey across the heavens each day. In the mountains of the east, there is a great doorway, tended by the scorpion-men left there by Tiamat, who is the great serpent of the abyss, the Goddess of Chaos. When the door is opened, Shamash emerges in all his fiery splendor. In his golden chariot, he ascends the mountain into the sky, and directs his course to the top of the heavens where he shines brightly at midday. As his path continues, he arrives at the great mountain to the west. At sunset, this glorious figure disappears behind the western peak, and night descends upon the earth.

As a god of the Sun, Shamash is also a giver of wisdom and insight. He is a god of divination. The soothsayers of ancient Babylonia greatly honored the Sun God, for it was from Shamash that they received the truth that they spoke. His great light illuminated not only the earth: for those with eyes to see, his light cast off the haze of darkness from the future, and gave clarity to those who sought to see the future.

Lucifer, Lord of Light

No book of the legends of the Sun would be complete without the inclusion of a word about Lucifer. While in our day Lucifer has become known as the devil, the alter-ego of Satan, he has not always been seen in this manner. He originated as a much more likeable character.

Lucifer first emerged as a solar figure. His Hebraic name is *Helel ben-Shahar*, which means Day Star, Son of the Dawn. In Latin, his name means "bearer of light." This is far from the image of the demonic entity that his name invokes today.

So how did this divine being of light, the personification of the Sun, fall from grace? The answer cannot be found in mythology, but in the history of the world at the time the legend of Lucifer's fall was created.

In order to take a firm foothold among the people, Christianity, which was a new religion at the time, had to uproot the old pagan beliefs. Lucifer's fall is a part of the beginning of this campaign, since Lucifer symbolizes the old Pagan ways of worship.

In this new mythology, Lucifer's divinity is acknowledged. But rather than the leader of the pagan pantheon, he becomes the leader of the fallen angels. The great crime of Lucifer was not his failure to subjugate himself before the new God—his fall from grace was due to his refusal to worship Adam. In other words, by making the old gods inferior to humanity, Christianity made people look elsewhere for the divine light of the Sun.

Lucifer is also associated with the serpent in the garden of Eden. It was Lucifer that was held responsible for enticing Eve to pick the apple from the tree and gain the knowledge of good and evil. You would not think this to be a capital offense. Yet in bestowing knowledge upon the first man and the first woman, Lucifer committed an offense deemed unforgivable by the new God.

Yahweh, the Judeo-Christian God, had directly forbidden Adam and Eve from partaking of the fruit of knowledge. By directing Eve to disobey this order, Lucifer directly challenges the authority of the new regime. Yahweh's punishment is swift—Adam and Eve are barred from the Garden of Eden, and the serpent becomes the lowliest and most hated of creatures. Hence, the Lord of Light becomes the Prince of Darkness, and is thereafter associated with Satan.

Although more widely recognized, and more readily available, the Christian tales of Lucifer are not the only legends concerning the Lord of Light. In fact, in other legends, Lucifer is actually exalted after his "fall from grace." In Charles G. Leland's *Aradia: Gospel of the Witches,* Lucifer is portrayed as God of the Sun and Moon, and the God of Light. He is a god full of splendor, a pleasure to look upon, and very proud of his beauty.

Diana, Goddess of the Moon and sister to Lucifer, adored her brother. In time, they had a girl-child together, whom they named Aradia.

At this time, it seems that the wealthy had become the oppressors of those who were less fortunate. They enslaved them, controlled them, and mistreated them. It was the mission of the daughter of Lucifer and Diana to restore some note of balance to the world. It was given to Aradia to punish the oppressors and lift the fortunes of the oppressed. Like a Robin Hood of the spirit, the daughter of Lucifer stole from the evil men of wealth and gave to those who had no material goods, but knew a richness in their souls.

So stands Lucifer, Lord of Light, Prince of Darkness, lover of life, Demon Serpent of Evil, benefactor of those who are oppressed by evil. In the personage of Lucifer is embodied all opposites. He is messenger of truth, granter of goodness, or he is the embodiment of evil and the ruler of hell. He is the bright Sun at midday, and he is the darkest hour of night.

Huitzilopochtli, God of Blood and Fire

In the legendry of the Aztec people, the Sun God Huitzilopochtli was born wearing the raiment of the sky, fully armored and ready for battle. He was clad in blue armor, held a blue spear in his mighty hand, and wore a headdress of blue hummingbird feathers on the left side of his head. In the Aztec language, his name is descriptive of his appearance, meaning "Blue Hummingbird on the Left."

The Aztec culture was an often violent one. This is well reflected in the tales of their deities. Huitzilopochtli was a bloodthirsty god. His first act as Sun God was to slay his sister Coyolxauhqui and his four hundred brothers for scheming against their mother, Coatlicue. From his worshippers below, Huitzilopochtli demanded human sacrifice to his honor.

Paradoxically, in his aspect as Xochipilli, the Sun God also showed a kinder, more humane side as the guardian of souls and lord of the flowers. In his temple, he was made offerings of food, flowers, and sweet-smelling incense.

Nevertheless, his violent nature was predominant by far. When the Aztecs set out on their conquest of Mexico, it was under the leadership and for the honor of the Sun God, who told them that war and conquest was his goal. Even when their conquest was complete and the Aztec civilization was in its full glory, the bloodthirsty Huitzilopochtli was the inspiration of further bloodshed. The Aztecs continued to attack. One of their main objectives in continuing conflict was to gain lives to sacrifice to their Sun God.

This bloody practice sometimes reached epic proportions. In the dedication of the newly erected Temple of the Sun in their capital city, the Aztecs sacrificed an estimated 70,000 lives to Huitzilopochtli. Each victim was led up the steps of the Sun Temple. When their ascent was complete, they were sacrificed to the Sun God in the traditional way, by having their hearts torn out by the priests of Huitzilopochtli.

There are some deities with power that seem to transcend the boundaries of their own cultures and exert control even over those who have roots in other religions and different ways of life. Such is the case with the Aztec Sun God. When the Spaniards arrived in the lands of the Aztec, they were appalled at the butchering of innocents in the name of Huitzilopochtli. These Christian visitors were horrified at the useless and brutal deaths in the name of a deity, and set out to purge the land of this evil. In so doing, they gave the greatest honor to the Aztec Sun God. In order to make this primitive land a place acceptable to all "right-thinking" men and women, they rid the land of these purveyors of human abomination by means of the sword and the flame. Death by blood and fire—an offering most sacred to Huitzilopochtli.

Ra, Father of Kings

One of the most widely recognized Sun Gods is the Egyptian creator-god, Ra. He was known by many names through the changing dynasties of the great Egyptian civilization. At different times Ra was worshiped as Atum-Ra, Khepri, Re, Re-Herakhty, and Amon-Re. His manifestations were as varied as his names. Ra is seen in *ben-ben*, the stone obelisk erected by Pharaoh Senusert I. He is seen in the mythical Benu, an Egyptian fire bird not unlike the phoenix. Ra is formless, and he is a child perched upon the throne of a king. He is the sacred bull known as "Merwer," and he is seen making his daily journey in the Sun barge across the sky.

Like other Sun Gods, Ra is in constant conflict with the forces of darkness. At each day's end he is swallowed by Apep, the demon serpent of darkness. During the day, Apep has little power over the Sun God. However, the conflict between these two opposing forces is eternal. The night beast is sometimes apparent during the day when he raises storm clouds to veil the brilliance of Ra. Each night, the dark creature succeeds in swallowing the Sun God. But in the dawn, Ra emerges victorious once more, reborn as a child of light.

The Pharaoh Chephren was the first Egyptian ruler that referred to himself as the "Son of Ra." However, the legends suggest that the Sun God was, in fact, the father of all the pharaohs. Whenever a new pharaoh was to be born, it is said that the glorious Ra lay down with the queen of the land. It is this that gives the ancient rulers the right to claim divine lineage. It is this that makes the Egyptian Sun God the sire of kingly children.

Odhinn, One-Eyed Warrior

Odhinn, also known as Odin, Woden, Wotan, and Witan, is the Norse/Teutonic Sun God. His name is descriptive of his character as well as his solar domain. The Germanic word *wuten* means to rage. Like the blazing fires of the Sun, so potent is the warrior god's battle fury.

Befitting a lord of the Sun, Odhinn is often pictured garbed in the dress of a warrior, his armor forged in the sacred metal of solar deities. He wears a breastplate of pure gold. On his head is a golden-horned helmet. His weapon is the golden spear forged magically by dwarfs, and he rides an eight-legged horse across the sky.

As a warrior lord, Odhinn is served by the Valkyries, warrior maids who participate in every earthly battle and determine its outcome. He is also the inspiration behind the famed berserkers, warriors crazed with the fury of the battle, drunk with zeal, and almost unstoppable in their rampage of death.

The Sun God has but one eye. It is said that he gave the other for the gift of magic mead, a drink of poetic inspiration and knowledge. Odhinn plucked his eye from its socket and dropped it into the well of Mimir, that he might drink from the magic waters and gain infinite wisdom.

The great inspiration of the enchanted well must have certainly had its effect on the warrior. He became known as a great healer, and as the God of Poetry. Still, he retained his position as the Sun God, and in his battle fury, he was known as the One-eyed Warrior.

Vulcan, Luciferian Sun

*A*lthough not as widely recognized as those of his fellow deities of the great Greco-Roman pantheon, the tales of Vulcan have been highly favored in English literature. Perhaps this is because Vulcan represents a cross-over figure between the old pagan ways and the newer schools of Christian thought. Arising from the ancient Roman empire (Rome being the center of the Christian religion and modern-day home of the Roman Catholic church), Vulcan's role as a transitionary god becomes significant.

Vulcan is a solar deity. His rule is over all forms of fire. The raging fires of devastation are his, as well as the fires of the Sun. His too is the hearth fire, a flame benevolent to humankind.

There is a story told of Vulcan's banishment from the domain of the gods, a story that reflects the daily course of the Sun. When Vulcan is cast down from the divine kingdom by the father of the gods, it takes him a full day to land. From the first of the day until noon, Vulcan soars up across the sky. At noon, he reaches the midpoint of the heavens. From midday until sunset, he continues his descent. Then, at last, he comes to rest in the west on the isle of Lemnos in the Aegean Sea.

In his exile from the kingdom of gods, Vulcan's legend parallels that of Lucifer. Vulcan's mother Juno had a row with her husband Jove, who was the great King of Heaven and Father of the Gods. Vulcan took his mother's side in the dispute, and Jove cast him down in a fit of rage. Like Lucifer, Vulcan had the audacity to stand against the King of Heaven, and like him, was cast down from heaven. Both were punished by an enraged supreme deity. Yet, the great rage that leads to the banishments, the loss of control, is that of the King of Heaven. Who is it who acts out of righteousness, and who out of pride?

Once revered as Sun God, Lord of Lightning and Thunderbolt, the greatest of the workers of metal, designer and builder of the great structures of Olympus, Vulcan is now reduced to a household deity through his exile. Vulcan became the God of the hearth, the patron of the smith. While a beneficial deity in the realm of the mundane, there is a majesty that has been forgotten. Yet those who know his legend still recognize Vulcan as God of the Sun in all his brilliant sovereignty.

Dahzbog, Lord of Rebirth

The Slavic deity Dahzbog is fascinating in many of his characteristics. He is actually a "second generation" deity, inasmuch as his rise to prominence was a new innovation in the religious and mythological conceptions of his culture. At one time, the Slavic people addressed their worship directly to the creator Svarog, a sky god. As the story develops, Svarog is credited with having two children. They are Dahzbog, the Sun, and his younger brother Svarogich, fire.

Time passes, and the concept of the two children loses favor. At this point, the story is born that Svarogich burns himself up in his own splendid flames. The younger god then vanishes from the Slavic legends, leaving his brother the Sun God as the primary deity.

As the popularity of Dahzbog increases, he becomes not only the offspring of Svarog, but his replacement. It is now Dahzbog who is identified as the creator. He becomes known as the Father of Sun and Fire.

The legend of the daily rise and fall of Dahzbog mirrors the tales of many other Sun deities—but with an important twist. Whereas many of the Sun deities make their daily journey across the sky each day, then vanish into the west, Dahzbog actually endures a daily cycle of birth, death, and resurrection.

The image of the rise and fall of the Slavic Sun God each day is reminiscent of the tales of his counterparts in other cultures, and portrays as majestic a vision as they. It is said that far away beyond the eastern horizon is the land of eternal summer. Within its boundaries stands a splendid palace made of gold. Every day, the Sun God is born and emerges from the palace in a chariot pulled by white horses, great in strength and with breath of fire.

As his mighty steeds draw his chariot to the top of the sky, Dahzbog increases in his own majesty and glory. At noon, when he rides the height of the heavens, he is in his fullest glory—King of the Heavens.

From this point, the downward journey has begun. Dahzbog wanes in his brilliance. As he nears the farthest reaches of the western sky, the kingdom of death, he succumbs to the age of the day, and he dies. Each new dawn, Dahzbog is born anew, and his journey to glory is repeated.

The year of the Sun God is as rich with rejuvenation as is his day. Every summer, Dahzbog marries Myesyats, Goddess of the Moon. Together, they give birth to many children. These are the stars. When summer comes around again, there is yet another wedding night, and the stars are reborn in the sky.

Dahzbog is reported to have great wealth and power. He is lord over twelve different kingdoms. These are kingdoms of the sky—the twelve signs of the zodiac.

And so the ancient cycle continues. Each sunset, we remember Dahzbog as he enters the land of death. When each new day arises, we await the golden child who emerges from the eastern palace of gold.

Apollo, Olympian Bard

Although a Sun God, Apollo had great talents that are not as often noted as his dominion over the life-giving light. He was an artisan, a poet, a musician, as well as a Greek solar deity. The handmaidens of Apollo are known to us as the nine Muses, from whom all inspiration arises.

From ancient Greece come tales of a time when Apollo was banished by Zeus to the lands of King Admetus of Pherae for the murder of Cyclopes. Apollo slew Cyclopes because he had developed the thunderbolt, which was the weapon used to slay Asclepius, Apollo's son.

In the service of King Admetus, Apollo knew peace and humility. He was most often seen in the company of the Muses, playing sweet music on his lyre. Apollo was the inventor of the lyre, and unequalled in its playing. So melodious were the sounds he produced that even the wildest of beasts were soothed by his songs.

As a poet and musician, Apollo cannot be divorced from the arena of the heart. His love affairs were many. But perhaps there are none so well remembered as his love for the maiden Daphne, daughter of the river god Peneus.

Apollo adored the maiden, and had to have her. He looked at her with her hair flowing in lovely disarray over her white shoulders. He saw the brightness in her innocent eyes, no less endowed with light than the stars in the heavens. His heart full of love for the maiden, his eyes burning with passion, he approached Daphne to be as one with her. The maiden, frightened of his advance, took flight from him.

Apollo entreated Daphne to end the chase. He explained that it was not for ill intent that he pursued her, but for the glory of love. Still, she continued to run from him in fear. With his love to inspire him, Apollo quickened his pace and began gaining on the girl. As he was almost upon her, his divine breath touched her hair. Touched by the breath of Apollo, the strength began to drain from Daphne, and the chase was all but over. She could not continue her flight.

In a last desperate effort to escape the passion of the god, Daphne called for the aid of her father. "Peneus," she shouted. "Open the earth to swallow me up that I may be free from the advances of Apollo, or else change this beauteous form to something less desirable!"

With that, Daphne's arms and legs began to stiffen. Her soft figure became enclosed in bark. The lovely hair that Apollo had so admired turned into leaves. Her arms became branches. When Apollo saw the sudden transformation, he was amazed. He stood a long time and examined the tree. He gently brushed the leaves that were once her hair. He felt the bark that had been her tender flesh, and he grieved his loss.

Although Apollo could never have Daphne as she was, his love for her never totally subsided. The laurel tree that the maiden had become became the sacred tree of the Sun God. He wore a crown of laurel leaves, and in Daphne's honor the laurel was woven into wreaths to adorn the greatest sons of Rome. Conquering heroes would be adorned with laurel upon their successful return home, and poets were awarded with laurel wreaths to celebrate their artistry and inspiration.

And so the great Apollo, God of the Sun, lord of poetry and music, is patron to those who love and dream. He watches over them as the Sun watches over the day.

Lugh the Long-Handed

Among the Irish people, the legends of the *Tuatha de Danaan*, the people of the goddess Danu, are highly favored by story-tellers These are the tales of adventure, romance, and magic of the Irish Celts.

One of the principal deities of the Tuatha is Lugh, the Sun God. His adventures in Irish mythology were many. Clad in helmet and armor of gold, he made his way through the Irish countryside, a vision of valor, wisdom, and beauty. Lugh was all that might be expected in the person of a divine being, and that to which all might aspire. He is God, hero, and the essence of what human potential could attain.

This Celtic Sun God receives his name from one of his best-remembered adventures. From this adventure he is called Lugh Lamhfhada, the Long-Handed, a title borne of the tale of his confrontation with Balor, the legendary demonic giant of Celtic mythology.

Balor was a great and terrible figure. It was said that four men were required to open the lid of the giant's evil eye. Once opened, any who stood within its view was instantly killed. For this reason, the evil giant king was called Balor of the Baleful Eye.

According to legend, it was during the second battle of Moytura that this great confrontation occurred. This was when the Tuatha de Danaan faced the Formorians, the tribe of which the dread Balor was king. During the battle, the lid of the terrible eye was lifted. Many Tuatha warriors were slain as the evil eye caught them in its fatal gaze. Lugh, however, remained outside the range of the terrible eye. After it had done its worst, and claimed the lives of many of his companions, Balor's eyelid grew weary, and began to close.

Before the heavy eyelid could be lifted once more and the terrible eye fix its deadly gaze upon the golden warrior, Lugh fixed a stone in his sling, and let it fly toward the evil eye of the giant. Lugh's arm was strong, and his aim was true. Just as it was about to open, the stone pierced through the great eye and into the brain of Balor. In an instant, the terrible Balor was no more. Thus Lugh, in honor of his conquest and for his skill and mastery with his sling, was remembered as the Long-Handed.

Another name by which we remember the gold-clad Lugh is Samildanach, or God of All Arts. This name arises from the tales of another of Lugh's many adventures in the legendry of the Tuatha de Danaan. It is from the time when Lugh sought entry into the court of Nuada, king of the Tuatha de Danaan.

Lugh arrived at the gates of the palace of Nuada in Tara, the capital city of the Tuatha. The gatekeeper stopped him, and asked his profession. "No one is admitted through this gate," he said, "unless he is a master of his craft." To this, Lugh replied, "I am a master carpenter." Said the gatekeeper, "As excellent as you may be, Luchtaine dwells beyond these gates. There is no greater carpenter than he. We have no need of another."

"I am a most able smith," said Lugh. "As is the noble Goibniu," replied the gatekeeper. "We have no need of another.

"I am a champion warrior," Lugh reported, "known for skillfulness as well as strength." "Ogma is our champion," explained the man at the gate. "We need no other."

Lugh went on speaking of his virtues one by one. "I am a bard," he said. "I am a harpist, a magician, a physician, a worker of bronze." Each new skill Lugh described was met with the name of another within the palace whose mastery of the craft was equal to his own. And each time Lugh was denied entry beyond the gates.

At long last, Lugh said, "Go and ask your king if he has such a man within the palace who is master of all these skills at once, for if he does, there is certainly no use for me to ride beyond these gates." This message was brought to Nuada. In reply, the king sent his finest chess player to challenge Lugh. In a short time, Lugh easily defeated this master, whereupon he was admitted into the court of Nuada.

Once within the palace walls, each of the great masters of Tara challenged this youth who claimed mastery in their particular area of expertise. One by one, the young Lugh bested each of the masters in their own craft. All agreed to the depth of his skill in each of the crafts, and accepted him as a master of all things. It is because the young Lugh was successful in mastering the masters that he is yet known as God of All Arts.

Ladies of Light

*T*hroughout the world there are also many examples of Sun Goddesses that have had their time of reign in the sky. Their legends are refreshing, not only for the novelty of female dominance in an area commonly considered under the jurisdiction of the male, but for the different virtues they bring to the kingdom of the Sun—qualities that can best be expressed in the form of a female deity.

The deep, abiding love of motherhood and the sensual enchantments of a lover are among her gifts to the life-giving qualities of the Sun. Her feminine nature adds fullness to the considerations of the solar deity. To the region of the mind, wisdom, and intellect, she adds dreams and inspiration. To courage and valor she brings compassion. The hard edge of justice is tempered by her understanding.

However, though many are the differences, so do the Gods and Goddesses of the Sun share some common ground. They are each majestic in their shining glory. One is no less regal than the other. Neither is less worthy of the power they wield or the adoration they receive. In strength, the Sun Goddess is no less impressive a vision than her masculine counterparts. As a warrior goddess, be assured she is no less competent, no less fierce in battle than the Sun Gods of other cultures. Should the situation arise wherein she has to mete out punishment, her justice will be delivered with no less swift a hand than that of a male deity.

As the Sun Gods are undoubtedly deserving of their title of Lord, so the Solar Goddesses of such royal and divine nature are most appropriately considered Ladies of Light.

Hae-Sun, the Sun Maiden

The Sun Goddess of Korea presents an image of innocence. It is Hae-Sun's child-like virtues that give the Sun its brilliance. And, in fact, Hae-Sun begins her life as a Sun Goddess as a mere child.

Hae-Sun was one of three children. One sister, Dael-soon, was the Moon. Her other sister, Byun-soon, was a star. It is said that of the three, Hae-Sun was the shyest. When she first began her trek across the sky as the Sun, everything was fine. After a time, however, she noticed that the people below were staring at her. This made the young maiden very self-conscious. She continued her journey across the sky, but as she did, glowed brighter and brighter in her embarrassment. As she did, her light became blinding, and the people below were no longer able to look directly upon her. This suited the modest girl quite well, and the Sun has been glowing brightly ever since.

One of the most fascinating legends of the Korean Sun Goddess is about how she came to be the Sun. Hae-Sun actually began as a mortal child. She only came to dwell in the heavenly abode of the gods through the mighty ones' compassionate aid to an innocent child in need. This tale is especially noteworthy to the Western reader, since it seems as though it is almost an Eastern translation of the fairy tale of Little Red Riding Hood. The wolf becomes a tiger, a beast far more at home in Korea, and the symbolic divine intervention of the woodcutter becomes actual divine intervention. Other than that, the tales are similar, even down to the "box of goodies."

One day, Hae-Sun's mother was coming home from the market. Along the way she met a tiger, who inquired about the contents of the box she carried under her arm. "It is buckwheat pancakes, one for each of my three daughters who await my return," replied the woman. "Then give me one, or I shall have to devour you!" demanded the tiger. Needless to say, there was no delay in delivering the pancake to the tiger.

Believing herself safe, Hae-Sun's mother began to hurry home. But as she rounded a turn in the path, she found another tiger standing there, as if awaiting her arrival. The scene was repeated, and the second of her three pancakes was gone.

Now, unbeknownst to the girls' mother, the second molester was really not a new beast at all. The tiger had taken a shortcut and gotten to the bend in the path ahead of her. Since all that one ever notices about a tiger up close is the sharp, threatening teeth, all tigers do tend to look alike at close range.

Having satisfied the hungry tiger and watched him disappear into the woods, Hae-Sun's mother stepped up her pace to get home to her daughters. As might be expected, round another bend she came upon what seemed to be a third tiger demanding her final pancake. Again, she complied and watched him go off into the woods.

Upon their next meeting, there were no more pancakes to offer the tiger, and Hae-Sun's mother became an unfortunate victim of the tiger's endless hunger. The tiger now dressed in the woman's clothing and hurried along to the house where her children awaited her arrival.

Knocking at the door of the house, the tiger called out, "Children, unlock the door! It is your mother home from market." "You don't sound like Mother," shouted back Hae-Sun. "Why, I've lost my voice from shouting, trying to sell our vegetables at the market," the Tiger answered.

Dael-Soon looked out from a tiny hole in the door of the house. Through it, she saw one big red eye. "That does not seem to be the eye of our mother," the girl said. "It is far too big and far too red!" "Some red pepper blew into my eye at the marketplace. It is quite red and swollen. Please let me in so that I may tend to it."

Byun-Soon did not believe the voice on the other side of the door. She said, "Place your hand through the window. By this, we will know you for certain." The tiger thrust an orange paw through the window, and the girls knew that this was not their mother.

Already prepared with a lie as to why this hand did not look like the soft hand of the girls' mother, the tiger was surprised when a voice called through the door, "Just a moment, Mother. We will let you in!" Pleased that the plan had worked, the tiger confidently waited for the door to open. He could almost taste the flesh of the young girls as he stood there.

In the meantime, the three sisters, well aware of the danger, hurried out the back door and scurried up a tree. The tiger tired of waiting and broke down the door that had kept him from his dinner. Inside, there was no trace of the three young sisters. Seeing that the back door was ajar, however, the tiger looked out and saw the girls perched high in the tree.

With the hungry Tiger preparing to climb, the three frightened sisters turned the only way they could for hope. Looking into the heavens, the children prayed, "If we are to live, send us a strong iron chain to carry us to safety. If our days are ended, then send a weak straw rope, and we will plunge to the open jaws of our pursuer!" A strong chain appeared from the sky, and the girls climbed into the heavens, far from the Tiger below.

And that is how Hae-Sun and her sisters came to dwell in the land of the gods. Each became, in time, a being of light, but Hae-Sun shone most brightly as the Korean Goddess of the Sun.

Yhi, Giver of Light and Life

The Aboriginal Sun Goddess is called Yhi. She is an impressive figure, combining the majesty of the Sun with the softness of a woman. Yhi shines as powerfully as her male counterparts, yet knows a tenderness that escapes many of the Sun Gods.

According to the legends of the Aborigines, Yhi is responsible for much of the work of the creation. Hearing the whispered desires of Baiame, the Great Spirit, Yhi descended to the earth. The Sun Goddess left her mark wherever she went, like footprints in sand. As her heat passed over the land, it became alive and fertile. Flowers, trees, and plains colored the brown earth as they were touched by her golden rays. As she rested from her first efforts of creation, Yhi was pleased with all that she saw. From the soft whispers of the Great Spirit carried on the breezes, she knew that Baiame also approved of her efforts.

Next, the Sun Goddess journeyed to the dark places beneath the earth. As she did, life began to stir all about her. Newly born insects followed their creator from out of the dark places into the outer world. They immediately set about their work, pollinating the flowers and helping the seeds of new trees to fall to the earth where they began to sprout with new life.

Yhi then traveled to the snow-capped mountains. As she neared the frozen peaks, her heat began to melt the ice into fine streams running down the mountainsides. Within the flowing waters, life began to form. Fish and reptiles, snakes and turtles were born. As the ice and snow continued to melt, streams became rivers, and rivers pooled into clear lakes teeming with the life of the water creatures.

The Sun Goddess entered into the caves cut into the sides of the brown rock of the mountains, where she found the sleeping souls of the creatures of the air and the four-legged beasts of the soil. Awakened by the brilliant light of Yhi, the birds stirred and then took to the air. The land creatures woke up too, and ran freely down the rocky slopes.

When all this was done, Yhi welcomed the newly born creations to the outer world. She told them that this was to be their home, and wished them happiness. She told them that they were under the watchful eye of the Great Spirit who would love and protect them, and bid them farewell, for the time had come for her to leave them for her home in the sky.

As the Sun Goddess ascended the sky, her great light began to fade until she disappeared over the western horizon. At first, the creatures were fearful of the darkness that came in her absence. Then, after a time, the birds heralded her return over the eastern edge of the world. The creatures were comforted by her return, and she explained that her time with them was limited, but that she would always return to light the world each day.

Still, Yhi was a compassionate goddess. In order to allay their fears when darkness fell, she placed the Morning Star, known to us as Venus, in the sky. To keep this single luminary from becoming lonely, Yhi created the Moon, called Bahloo. Bahloo gave birth to other stars, and the night became a display of sparkling majesty.

It seemed that the work of the creation had gone well. Baiame and Yhi were pleased—until one day when the Sun Goddess returned to her creatures. They had become jealous of one another. The land creatures wanted wings. Birds wished to explore the waters like fish. Fish wanted to walk and run like land creatures.

Saddened by the demands of her creations, and disappointed in their inability to appreciate their own virtues, Yhi returned to her home in the sky. She left the resolution of this dilemma to Baime, the Great Spirit.

Baiame was displeased when he heard the demands of the creatures. In his anger, he sent a great flood to the land. The birds and beasts hid in the caves, fearful for their safety. The fish and water creatures dove deep beneath the water, scared and trembling.

When the flood waters subsided, Yhi came back to warm the earth. Slowly, the animals withdrew from their hiding places. When they emerged, they were met by a new creature.

While they huddled together far from the destructive waters, Baiame had been making a creation of his own. Now, standing before them, the creatures met the soul of the Great Spirit himself, enshrined in the body of Man.

The legend tells us that Man was placed upon the earth to rule over the animals. This he has done from the very beginning. In time, however, Man learned loneliness. Although he had come to love the creatures placed beneath his rule, they had a soul unlike his own, and he could not feel as one with them.

One morning, Man awoke to discover Yhi shining brightly upon a certain yacca tree. As he watched the tree, alive with the brilliance of the Sun Goddess, it began to change form before his eyes. The yacca tree developed into a form similar in shape to his own, yet somehow different. It was more rounded, more graceful, and had a softness that was pleasurable, yet foreign to him. From the yacca and Yhi's light Woman was born, and stepped from the tree to join with Man.

All of creation was happy. The wisest of the creatures remember the time of the flood, and have come to appreciate the virtues given to them by the Sun Goddess. Man and Woman delight in each other's embrace, while high above it all Yhi watches over this happy scene and is pleased with her creation.

Sulis' Healing Waters

*I*n many cultures, the Sun represents the force of life and the power of health and healing. In Britain, this association takes on a different expression. Sulis, though undoubtedly a Sun Goddess, does not heal through the power of the Sun directly, but through the magic of the hot springs endowed with her solar virtue.

The healing hot mineral waters in southwestern England at Bath are sacred to Sulis. It is believed that the priestesses of Sulis honored her in this place by tending an eternal flame that reflected and revered the great fires of the Sun. Her followers were bathed in the sacred, life-giving waters of the springs.

To some extent, we can only wonder of the exact nature of the events at Bath in the days of Sulis. During the Roman occupation of Britain, her shrine was dutifully tended by the Roman conquerors. When the sons of Rome left the sacred lands of the Sun Goddess, however, flood waters that were a constant threat to the site overcame the land. The temple of Sulis collapsed into the mud. The healing pool itself became little more than a swamp.

Still, there have been some hints about this shrine of the Sun Goddess. Archaeologists have conducted a series of excavations at the site, uncovering the great temple of Sulis, among other artifacts. A likeness of the goddess in bronze was found, along with various inscriptions to the goddess left in stone by her devotees.

Among the more interesting finds were Roman coins in the area of the great fountain at Bath. This evokes images of the sons and daughters of Rome tossing their tokens into the magical waters of Sulis. Even today, there are unwitting practitioners of the ancient rites. The next time we see a child toss a penny into a fountain to gain a wish, it will bring back visions of the children of the Sun Goddess making their offerings to Sulis, that she might grant them the blessings of her healing waters at Bath.

The Mourning Sun

Cherokee storytellers remember the Sun as Unelanuhi. She is also addressed as *Aaghu Gugu*, "beautiful woman." Though a principal deity of the Cherokee, and most reverently honored, there was a time when the people of the earth made plans to slay the goddess.

As the tale has been passed down through successive generations of native storytellers, the Sun Goddess was not always beneficial to the tribe. Although Unelanuhi made her daily pass across the heavens, she was not very concerned with the needs of the people. She had her own life beyond the desires of the puny race below. This was where her attention lay.

The Sun Goddess had a daughter to whom she was devoted. Unelanuhi's daughter had a small house that sat at the pinnacle of the sky. Every day at dawn, the loving mother would head out toward her daughter's house, arriving at midday.

As Unelanuhi approached the top of the heavens where her daughter lived, she would look down at the people of the land below. They, in turn, would return her gaze. However, the intensity of her radiance was blinding to the eyes of the earth people. Like us, they could not regard her without tightly squinting their eyes.

Unelanuhi looked down at the little squinty-eyed humans, and thought that they must be about the ugliest creatures she had ever seen. She thought the world would be better rid of this unseemly race, and determined to eliminate them. Every day from her daughter's abode in the heights of the sky she blazed down upon the people below. Her heat was so intense that the creatures below were beginning to succumb to it. Each day, a few more of the men and women of the tribe would die from the overpowering heat of the Sun Goddess.

It was the Spirit People who first counseled the tribe in their course of action. Unless the tribe took action to kill the goddess, they all would perish beneath her fiery gaze. Two of the people took the forms of snakes and set out to slay Unelanuhi. Up to the heavens they went, one as an adder, the other as a copperhead. They hid near the tiny house at the sky's peak and awaited the arrival of the Sun Goddess.

As the Sun approached, the snakes prepared to strike. Her dazzling light, however, blinded them and they were unable to hit their mark. When the treachery of these creatures was discovered, Unelanuhi chastised them and sent them slinking away in shame.

A second attempt was made to take the life of the goddess and end the scorching heat upon the earth. Two more people were transformed into snakes, but this time, more deadly creatures were chosen. One serpentine assassin went forth as a rattlesnake, and the other as a giant monstrous snake known as the Uktena.

A little overzealous in his mission, and perhaps a little less than intelligent, the rattlesnake sprung at the first figure he saw. In less than a moment, Unelanuhi's daughter lay dead from his venom. The snakes, fearing the wrath of the goddess when she arrived at her daughter's house, fled quickly back to the earth.

When Unelanuhi returned to the sight of the slain girl's body, she began to wail. She shut herself in her daughter's house, and the first darkness descended upon the world. The lands that had first suffered in the stifling grasp of intense heat now began to freeze with the absence of the Sun.

Attempts were made to bring the daughter of the Sun Goddess back to life so that the Sun's mourning could be ended, and her warm glow return to the land. Each try was unsuccessful.

At last, the people tried to entertain the Sun Goddess with inspired tales, and with dancing, songs, and music. Unelanuhi never even slightly regarded the creative efforts of the people to gain her attention, but continued her mourning.

Suddenly, as if inspired by some unknown hand, a drummer altered his beat. The sudden shift startled the Sun Goddess, and she smiled at the creative efforts of those around her.

According to the legend, this is how the mourning Sun returned her light to the world. Yet each night when the earth is covered by a blanket of darkness, we remember the legend of the time we almost lost our Sun forever.

Beiwe, Finder of the Lost

In old Norway, the Sun Goddess was known as Beiwe. Like many of the other solar personages, the Norwegian goddess traversed the sky in a heavenly coach. But unlike the chariots of other cultures, which were often made of precious gold or shimmering silver, Beiwe mounted the sky in a sled made of reindeer antlers.

While the Sun Goddess was a deity of fertility, bringing the green life back through the snow as the arctic winter began to subside, she was particularly protective of her sacred animal, the reindeer. Her green plants were made to thrive, primarily so that the herds of reindeer cattle would be able to survive.

Beiwe was especially tied to the white reindeer. In her rites, it was often a white reindeer that was offered in sacrifice. Because she had a special fondness for the yet unborn reindeer fawn, it was only the female of the species, the potential mother, that was considered a suitable offering.

Properly prepared and dedicated to the goddess, the animal was given up to the Sun. Sometimes the rites of sacrifice were initiated to gain Beiwe's favor in dispensing some urgent need of her people. In other instances, this ritual observance was on the occasion of the solstice celebration. In either case, it was not uncommon to ask a special blessing of the Sun Goddess on behalf of the insane. It was held by some that insanity was often caused by the absence of the Sun during the long, harsh, arctic winters.

As Beiwe may shine a special light on those who have been lost from reason, so were all the world's lost wanderers dear to her. When a hunter or a herdsman became separated from his fellows, there was a certain rite that could be engaged to ask the blessing of the Sun Goddess to deliver him from his situation.

Taking a thin growth from the land, a lost follower would form the wood into a circle, a shape sacred to the Sun. This Sun ring would be offered up to the goddess with a prayer that she did not allow the darkness to envelop the wanderer until the vision of the tents of the campsite were seen to rise above the horizon.

Having rule over the lost might seem a jurisdiction unworthy of the divine. However, it should be remembered that the arctic lands were filled with nomadic tribes. Becoming separated from a moving campground was not an uncommon occurrence, and being left alone to face the harshness of a winter night was a mortal danger.

In the arctic north, the land without full daylight for half the year, the Sun was a prominent deity and a primary force in the survival of the tribes. Whether tending to the herds that would sustain her worshippers, or returning the lost souls to the bosom of the tribe's protective unity, the white reindeer goddess was welcomed as she made her daily journey in her sled of sacred reindeer's antlers.

Walu the Dreamer

A lthough the legends of the Sun's course across the sky are many and varied, they usually bear certain similarities to one another. Normally, the Sun deity travels a path across the sky and is forced to wrestle with the darkness in one form or another. Sometimes the darkness is a beast that vanquishes the light; sometimes it is only a temporary setback or impediment to the shedding of the Sun's rays on the earth. In either case, the Sun returns again each dawn, ready to relive the cycle.

From Australia arises a tale unlike many others. Walu, the Australian Sun Goddess, does not confront the darkness. Night falls in the land down under simply because the Sun tires and slips off to dreamland.

The story of the day begins with Walu asleep in a cave. In her slumber, her arms rest over her bright countenance. When she awakes, however, she unfolds her arms and her light is shed upon the world. By the end of day, she finds that she again grows weary. On the Island of Bralgu, off in the western horizon, Walu finds a comfortable place to lie down. She settles down, covers her face with her arms, and the earth is in darkness once again.

In addition to giving light to the world, the Australian Sun Goddess is a goddess of fertility and a creation goddess. When she first rose above the earth, she tenderly touched the land with her fingers of sunlight. Beneath her touch, plants and trees sprang up. Spirits appeared among the plant creatures. It was they who helped to continue the work of creation after the Sun Goddess' lead. They formed the lakes and rivers of the earth. They created animals and birds to live upon the green land and in the skies above the land.

Each day as she passed over the newly created life, she tended it with her light. Plants grew tall and healthy. Trees began to bear fruit. The animal life feasted on the fruit from the trees. Birds ate of the wealth of berries offered by tree and bush. The world was young and vibrant and full of life.

Each day Walu rises above the earth, pleased with the beauty and perfection of her creation. When she is finished with the task of nourishing the plants and creatures of her magnificent earth, she falls to dreaming, and the darkness enfolds her beloved earth. At the dawn, Walu rises again to love and nurture her creation. For Walu, each day has always held the same.

Amaterasu, the Rising Sun

Japan has long been known as the land of the rising sun. Perhaps it is because it lies on the eastern side of the world of human culture. Perhaps it is because their national flag boasts a red sun rising out of a white field. But whatever mundane reasons for their proud title, there are tales of the divine that inspire this name rooted in the farthest reaches of Japanese culture.

The Sun Goddess of Japan is known as Amaterasu. She is a vision of bright beauty and strength. She is armed with bow and arrow, and her black hair hangs down, bound with strands of five hundred sparkling jewels. She is the essence of the radiant Sun that showers the eastern lands with its golden light. This is as it was in the earliest days of mythological history, and how it is today. There was a time, however, when Amaterasu retreated from her devotion to giving her light to banish the darkness.

It was all due to the actions of her brother, Susanowo. The brother of the Sun Goddess was a dark, violent god, a god of destruction, neither well favored among the Gods, nor as forthright and noble as might be expected of a divine being. He was of an evil nature, and his actions often reflected it intensely. Indulging his violent rage, Susanowo destroyed the rice fields, desecrated the sacred grounds, and brought havoc and destruction wherever he passed. Amaterasu, in the meantime, continued with her divine duties, despite the shameful actions of her brother.

Finally, in an attempt to gain the notice of Amaterasu, Susanowo broke through the wall of the room where the Sun Goddess was tending to the weaving of garments for all of the divine realm. Amaterasu and the maidens she supervised were terrified. Amaterasu rose to her full stature to protect the maids from the violence of her brother, but there was no confrontation.

Instead, Susanowo went to the palace where his sister took her food and drink. He laid to waste the refuge of the Sun Goddess, and fouled her temple of sustenance and repose. For Amaterasu, this final act of evil was more than she could endure.

Ashamed of the lack of honor in her brother's violent actions, and deeply wounded by the hurt he had directed at her personally, the Sun Goddess sought to retreat from the world of gods and men. She went to her cave, the Heavenly Rock Dwelling, and shut herself tightly inside it. When she did, her radiance was withheld from the world, and all the lands became dark.

There were eight hundred deities in the heavens at this time, and not one of them underestimated the seriousness of the situation (except, of course, Susanowo). They immediately called a great council to discuss how they might entice Amaterasu to emerge from her cave and restore the light to the world. They met at the River of Heaven to devise a plan, and in time had agreed on the course of action to be taken.

The divine council directed the Smith God to construct a great mirror of polished iron. They commissioned the stringing of a strand of five hundred claw-shaped jewels like the ones that the goddess wore in her hair. They hung the mirror, a symbol of the radiance of Amaterasu, along with the strand of jewels and many other offerings from a sacred tree. They caused the cocks to crow loudly in praise of the Sun Goddess. Finally, all the eight hundred deities joined in ritual song to entice Amaterasu from the Heavenly Rock Dwelling.

It seems that it was inspiration, rather than well-laid plans, however, that finally lured the Sun Goddess from her cave. As the rites continued, Amanouzume, the Dread Celestial Woman, began to dance to the great delight of the gathered deities. She danced on and on, until the entire company, spurred on by her antics, began to laugh.

From within her cave, Amaterasu heard the sounds of the deities gathered outside. She had heard their songs of praise, and understood the loss that her absence would be for the world, but still had no intention of quitting her cave. However, when the sounds from outside her hiding place turned to those of merry-making instead of worry, she became puzzled. She opened the cave just a crack to discover the mysterious sounds of mirth that stirred without. When she asked the reason for the joyful laughter, she was told that the gods had found a goddess more radiant, more pure than she.

At hearing this disturbing announcement, Amaterasu opened up her hiding place the rest of the way and emerged from the darkness. When she did, one of the wise gods held up the iron mirror so that the Sun Goddess was met with her own reflection. Fascinated with the bright vision of her own beauty, the goddess came forth from the Heavenly Rock Dwelling. As she did, she was met by the strong hand of one of the gods pulling her forward, while another god blocked her retreat back into the darkness with a straw rope.

Her brother, the dark god Susanowo, was banished to the underworld. As the Lord of Darkness, he is well suited to his dark mission. Amaterasu, in the meantime, resumed her place in the heavens, and continues to shed her radiance upon the world of gods and men.

Saule's Betrayal

The coastal regions of the Baltic Sea was home to the Sun Goddess Saule. In legends and folk songs, the tales of the goddess have been preserved. There are many myths that endure to tell her story. One of the most memorable explains how the Sun and Moon came to travel their separate paths across the sky.

Not long after the world was born, Saule was wed to the Moon God, Meness. In the beginning, their lives and their lights were as one. Each morning, the Sun Goddess awoke her husband, and they traveled across the sky together, illuminating the earth for all plants and creatures, and for all men and women.

It was the springtime of their love, and the world reflected the songs of their hearts. The earth, warmed by the love of the pair, knew eternal warmth. The people who lived upon the earth knew peace and happiness, and lived in harmony with one another.

Saule and Meness had many children together, stars to grace the heavens with their splendid light. The brightest and most highly favored by the goddess was the one known as Saules Meita, the daughter of the Sun. The Sun maiden had many suitors from among the sons of the divine kingdom. Saule looked forward to the time when her daughter would choose one of these fine young lords for her own.

It has often been seen that treachery is born of desire. The sensuous Sun daughter was so desirable, so endowed with the virtues of beauty, that there were few men who were not dazzled by her enchantments. Among those hypnotized by the Sun maid's splendor was her own father Meness.

To lay his plot, Meness complained of getting weary of making the daily journey across the sky with his wife. He began to remain at home while Saule continued to make her heavenly passage each day. In truth, however, Meness was seeking a way to spend time with the illustrious Sun daughter away from the sight of her mother. His incestuous designs were finally realized when, in the absence of Saule, the lovely Sun daughter lay down with the Moon.

When the Sun Goddess returned from her day's journey across the sky, she immediately knew that all had not been as it should have while she was away. Not seeing her daughter anywhere about, she searched the lands of the sky to find her. As she searched, she began to realize the truth of what had happened. Saule knew that the Moon God had betrayed her trust, and stolen the Sun maid's innocence from her. For his treachery, Saule took up a sword and sliced at Meness. Her attack left scars across the face of the Moon that have lasted until this day.

When Saule again found her daughter, she never let her stray from her side. The Sun maid is the bright star that accompanies Saule when she rises at dawn. She is also seen at the day's end in the Sun's waning light. Thus does Saule constantly protect the violated girl from any further incestuous designs that may be harbored by Meness.

As for the daily outings that Sun and Moon would take together each day, those times of love were erased along with the goddess' trust in her husband. The two still make their daily crossings, but never as husband and wife, never as the divine lovers that once they were. Saule waits until Meness begins to disappear on the far side of the sky before she leaves her house.

On her own, estranged from her husband, Saule continues to light the world. Her image is one of beauty, strength, and independence. Her glory is not diminished by the betrayal of her heart. She is still a regal figure, and her image as a lone figure accentuates her brilliance rather than lessening it.

When all was well with her husband, Saule lived with him in a small house at the edge of the sky. The image of her after the "divorce," however, is far more heavenly a picture. She now lives in a castle, surrounded by a gate of elegant silver. She rises early and adorns herself with silver jewelry, a bright red dress, and silver shoes. When Saule is ready to begin her daily trip along the skyways, she steps upon her silver chariot and races away. Her chariot is pulled by wild horses with stars glittering on their backs.

Saule is also remembered as a weaver goddess. Her light is made a thread at a time. When her spindle is full, the Sun Goddess weaves the threads of light into a fine blanket of sunshine that covers the land. By this weaving and spinning, the light of the Sun is forever renewed. Should the Saule ever tire of her art, the light of the world will unravel, and the coarse fabric of darkness will replace her golden blanket of light.

Sakhmet, Goddess of Beer and Blood

To the reader of Egyptian mythology, the name of Hathor is a familiar one. She is known as the Sky Goddess, the Divine Cow. She is a Goddess of Love, Joy, Dance, and Music. However, in another aspect, Hathor is known as Sakhmet, the Powerful One, a Sun Goddess. In this less-than-gentle persona she is represented in the form of a lioness, and is a goddess of war, battles, and bloodshed.

Her legend begins in the heavenly court of the god Re, the Creator God, essence of the Sun. In the early days, Re was the ruler of the mortal as well as the divine. As the god began to grow old, there were those in the mortal cities who plotted against him. At the urging of Nun, the God of the Watery Abyss, Re sent out his eye, the Sun, to catch the conspirators. Nun suggested, "Let your Eye go out as Hathor to discover those that would raise their hands against you."

So it was undertaken to find the traitors. Re sent his powerful eye, the embodiment of the Sun, in the form of Hathor. Empowered with the Sun, and entrusted with the mission of avenging the Creator God, Hathor became known as Sakhmet, the Powerful One, and wasted no time in carrying out her task.

Sakhmet raced to the desert where the traitorous mortals had taken refuge. With a mighty rage, she descended upon the enemies of Re. By the time she was done, great numbers of them lay slain, the desert red with their blood.

When the divine vengeance was complete, Re thanked Sakhmet for her swift and able handling of the matter, but also noticed something in her manner that worried him, for the Sun Goddess seemed to relish the bloody destruction. Re feared that once having had a taste of the kill, Sakhmet would continue to hunger for the lives of mortals.

Re ordered the High Priest of Memphis to pound great quantities of bright red ocher into powdered coloring. This was mixed with vast amounts of beer brewed by servant girls. Re then ordered the fields to be flooded with the red beer. Thousands of vessels were emptied over the lands, until the fields were covered with the blood-red mixture.

When the dawn arrived, Sakhmet was ready to begin anew her battle with the mortals. She was empassioned to see their blood flood the land, like the waters of the Nile rising above its banks. When she arrived at the scene, she was surprised and delighted to find the lands bright with the blood of men. She cupped her hands and drank deeply of the crimson liquid. The red mixture pleased the goddess, though it did not allay her passion for killing mortals. However, it was not long until the beer took hold of the goddess' senses. She became quite drunk, and was unable even to see men clearly, much less butcher them.

When the effects of the beer waned, it took the passion for slaughter with it. Re welcomed her back to his court in the much gentler aspect as Hathor. Grateful for the return of her gentle aspect, Re made a decree that from that day onward, at each occasion of feasting, the goddess would be honored with intoxicating drinks.

So the next time you see a companion raise a glass sunward in a toast upon a festive occasion, know that the custom is to the glory of the Sun Goddess, Sakhmet.

Hsi Wang Mu of the Setting Sun

*I*n China, tales are told of a land of life and of death. It is a land that exists somewhere off to the western horizon, and is ruled by Hsi Wang Mu, the Goddess of the Setting Sun.

The Chinese believe in reincarnation. It is possible that the souls of men are installed in new bodies for the continuance of their earthly journeys. Of course, this is not the only possibility for the human spirit. There are some truly enlightened souls that go to dwell with Buddha in the Land of Extreme Felicity. This is a land of enchantment and fulfillment. There is no wish that goes ungranted, no desire that is not fulfilled. Of course, only the highest souls will reach the kingdom of the Buddha. Other souls, if they are those of honorable men and women, might go to the Kun-Lun mountain, the land of Hsi Wang Mu.

Kun-Lun mountain is the land of the Immortals. The palace of Hsi Wang Mu rises upon the peak of the mountain, nine stories high, constructed of jade and surrounded by beautiful gardens. Within the gardens of the Goddess of the Setting Sun grows the Peach Tree of Immortality.

For the soul that journeys to this western heaven, there will be endless banquets. Hsi Wang Mu, along with her husband, the August Personage of Jade, will host the festivities. Side by side with the immortals of all ages, the feast of Immortal Peaches will be shared by all. These will be served up by a woman aged, yet ageless, born in a time before time, yet vibrant with youth and beauty. The Goddess of the Setting Sun, Queen of Heaven will pile the table high with the sacred fruit.

Ushas, Maid of the Dawn

The ancient hymns of India's *Rig Veda* sing the praises of the Dawn Goddess Ushas. Hers is a image of beauty, purity, and glory. In Sanskrit, her name means, simply, "to shine." Ushas is a daughter of Heaven, a sister of Night, and was born in the sky. The ancient hymns praise her as the fairest of all lights. She and her dark sister alternately switch places in the sky in a never-ending cycle of day and night.

Although Ushas cannot be considered the totality of the solar luminary, she is inseparable from its rise and fall each day. The Goddess of the Dawn is embodied in the first light of morning. Each dawn, while the world below is still steeped in darkness, Ushas adorns herself in bright garments and ornaments her body with shimmering trinkets. When she has finished dressing her youthful figure in brilliance, Ushas uncovers her gleaming white breast, pours sunshine over her already shining body, and goes along the path of previous dawns, now long departed and forgotten.

Her chariot of light is pulled across the sky by purple stallions. Within her dazzling chariot, Ushas carries all the gifts she brings to our world. She carries the brightest blessings, health, riches, and all the wondrous bounty that sustains life and makes it ever better.

Ushas is infinitely pure, and ageless. She has been among us since the beginning of time, yet retains her youth and beauty throughout the passing centuries. Within her gleaming chariot, the Goddess of the Dawn also carries the greatest of miracles known to the people of the lands below—the gift of offspring. The most devout pray in earnest to Ushas for the gift of her brilliant light of enchantment that brings children to the people of the earth. As the Maid of the Dawn traverses the heavens each morning, she renews the day—but with the gift of fertility, she also renews the generations. Thus, she bestows both light and life.

Bast, the Cat Goddess

$\mathcal{M}$any of the Sun Goddesses of mythology are truly deities of light. As such, they often have associations with the Moon, either with a Moon deity who is a lover or husband, or else they are somehow responsible for the Moon's creation. Bast stands out as unusual in this respect, since she seems to have few ties to the Moon. Whereas many of the female solar deities were, at least to some degree, goddesses of light and life-giving, Bast the Cat Goddess was purely and completely a Sun Goddess.

Although she was essentially a benevolent goddess, Bast had a harsher, almost demonic side to her personality. She was a goddess of joy. Music and dance were her worship. In this, she appealed to that spark within the human soul that loves life, that adores the goodness of living, and lives life to its fullest extent.

On the darker side, or what became perceived as the dark side, Bast was also a goddess of pleasure. Her worshippers pursued their revelry with total abandon. They enjoyed licentious sexual experiences, perhaps to the point of what we would consider perversion. The pursuit of pleasure was an act of worship to their goddess. Although this may have been an acceptable and even expected mode of behavior during the height of the goddess' reign in the Fourth century B.C., as times and moral codes changed it came to be considered a dark or left-hand path.

The less compassionate side of Bast can also be seen in her handling of those who abused her sacred totem, the cat. Her felines were very highly revered. To kill this sacred animal, even by accident, would mean death by hanging, with little or no chance for reprieve.

Bast is remembered as the image of a priestess or regal lady with the head of a cat. In her hand she carries a sistrum, which is an ancient Egyptian musical instrument. She also holds a basket full of kittens, representative of her station as the protector of cats.

Considered a daughter of Ra, the Creator God, she is known as the primary defender of the great god against his only true enemy. Although Egyptian mythology is rich with tales of how Ra enlisted the aid of one deity or another to fight his enemies (not the least of whom were human), it was only Apep that was truly a threat to the Creator God.

Apep was a serpent who represented evil incarnate, all the dark forces of the world. This is the familiar tale of the ceaseless battle between good and evil, darkness and light. Bast was charged with the protection of Ra against the demon Apep. Perhaps it is because of this that the Cat Goddess is most highly favored by the greatest of the Egyptian hierarchy.

At her most benevolent, Bast brings good fortune, pleasure, and elation for her worshippers. In her harsher aspect, she is not one to approach without a healthy fear and respect. Such is the nature of the Egyptian Cat Goddess, favored daughter of Ra, Goddess of the Sun.

Part
Three

Other Tales

Other Tales

*I*n addition to the legends of creation and the adventures of the solar deities, there are many folk tales about the Sun that have been carried through time by the storytellers and elders of various cultures. In these stories, the Sun takes on different aspects. It is sometimes a hero, and sometimes a fool.

The legends are repeated for education, for entertainment, or perhaps simply out of tradition. In some cases, the tales are not the instrument of some greater purpose, but are told for their own sake. They sometimes embody the spirit of a culture—an expression of the pride and the essence of a particular people.

Like the fairy stories of some lands, the universal legends of the Sun may delight and enlighten children of many ages, whether they be child in fact, or child at heart.

These are tales that bring laughter to the lighthearted, insight to the intellectual, and dreams to the poetic. These are the tales that brighten the hearts and minds of the people, just as the Sun brings golden brightness to the lands of the earth.

The Sun and the Bat

Certain tribes in Africa recount the tale of the Sun and the Bat. It is a story that explains why you will never find these two together in the sky.

In the beginning of the world, the Creator called forth all creatures to receive their purpose in life. He summoned his messengers, and gave them a time in which to return so that all creatures would arrive before him together.

The agent appointed to summon the Sun was the Bat. This messenger was not very devout in his duty, and was easily distracted along the way. At last, after all other creatures had been assigned their duties, the Creator tired of waiting for the Sun. He sent the dove, one of his most trusted messengers, to find the Sun and return with him.

When the dove returned with the Sun, the king assigned the task of lighting the way so that people could walk about. This was hardly the most glorious task that could have been assigned, and the Sun was not pleased at having raised the anger of the king through the failure of the Bat to fulfill his mission. It was then that the Sun first developed a dislike for the Bat, and it was but a short time later that the Sun had an opportunity to have his revenge.

The Bat had taken a dwelling with his aging mother. In time, the frailty of age began to consume her. She became very ill, close to death. To help his ailing mother, the Bat summoned the antelope to prepare a medicine to restore her to health. After examining the symptoms of the mother Bat, the antelope shook his head sadly, and told the Bat, "I cannot help to sponge away this illness. Only the Sun has medicine powerful enough to restore the aging one to health."

So the Bat set out to seek the Sun's help for his dying mother. The Sun was surprised to see his enemy approaching, and received him coldly, without a word of welcome. "If you've something to say to me, Bat, then speak now."

The Bat explained his trouble to the Sun, and wasted no time in asking for the medicine for his ailing mother. The Sun replied that it was necessary to return to his house before the medicine could be prepared. "Go now," said the Sun. "Return to me at my house tomorrow."

Night fell over the land and all creatures went to sleep. Early the next morning, Bat began his journey to the Sun's house to retrieve the medicine. Before he reached his destination, however, he met the Sun upon the path. He requested the medicine for his mother, but the Sun replied, "I told you to meet me at my house, but you met me on the path as I begin my day's journey. Once I leave my house, I can not return until the day's journey is completed. Go back and meet me at my house tomorrow."

The Bat returned to his home, and started out the next day to find the Sun at his house. Again, he found that the Sun had already begun the day's journey, and had to return without the needed medicine. Each day, the Bat's journey to the Sun's house was begun anew, and each day the Bat was late and returned to his dwelling empty-handed. Finally, on the seventh day, the ailing mother died.

In his grief, the Bat announced, "The Sun has killed my mother! Had he made the medicine she needed, she would be well! The evil Sun alone is to blame for my grief. From this day forward, I shall no more look upon his evil countenance. I shall stir only in darkness. When the Sun appears, I shall hide myself. In the darkness, I shall mourn the beloved mother that the Sun has taken from life."

So has it always been that the Bat is seen only in the darkness. To this day, he avoids the Sun who walks the path during the day, and can be seen in the night, mourning his loss.

Children of the Sun

Among the Incan people, stories are told of how the great compassion of the Sun inspired him to send his offspring to dwell among the Incan forefathers. This was during a time not long after the beginning of time.

Now, when we look upon the lands that the Incan people have inhabited, we see fertile soil that yields rich crops to feed the people. Fresh waters flow from the mountains to nourish the green fields, and offer clear, clean refreshment to the thirst of the men and women who tend the fields.

The grasslands offer nourishment to the great flocks of llamas that are kept by the tribe.

It was not always so. When the Incan people were first set upon the earth, they lived in barren country. It was stark with cold rocks and forested with thickets. There was no fresh water from the mountains. They had no crops and tended no llamas. Their homes were made in caves, or they found shelter in holes dug in the cold ground. To nourish their bodies, they dug roots from the ground or fought with the beasts over the corpses of animals they had killed. To cover their bodies from the rain and wind they either pulled bark from trees, or went naked through the day. At nightfall, there were no warm blankets to cover them. They were alone and unprotected against the chill of the dark night. Indeed, it was quite difficult to survive. The demands of living through each day were such that ease and leisure were virtually unknown to the tribe.

When the Sun saw the trials of the Incan people, he set his son and daughter to live among them, so as to teach them better ways of living. The children of the Sun were set in a boat upon the waters of Lake Titicaca and instructed to travel until they arrived at the place where the people lived. To his son, the Lord Sun gave a golden staff. He told him to lead the people to a place where the earth was soft and fertile, and that he would know this place through the golden staff. "You will find a land," said the Sun, "where the staff will sink deeply when you place into the ground. This will be the new land of the people."

The children of the Sun dwelt long among the ancestors. They taught them how to live together as husband and wife, as family and tribe. Having brought the Inca together as one people, they now led them from the barren land in which they had found them.

As they journeyed, the son of the Sun would sometimes drop the golden staff into the soil. At times, it would hardly sink into the earth at all. Other times, it might sink to half its length. At last, they came to a place where, when the son of Lord Sun dropped his golden staff, the soft earth swallowed it up, until only the very top of the golden rod could be seen. This was the home for which they had been searching. It was here that the ancestors of the Incan people made their home and built their cities.

The children of the Sun showed the people how to plant crops in the rich soil, and how to lead the water from the mountain streams to irrigate their fields. They taught the people how to build strong houses for shelter, and how to tame llamas, and to fashion their wool into garments for the people to wear and fine blankets to keep them warm. The tribe learned how to work in gold and silver, and to make pots and water vessels from clay.

Life was much better for the Incan people than when the son and daughter of the Sun had first come to live among them. The tribe was grateful for the goodness that had been brought to them. They were pleased for their bounty and for the benevolence of the children of the Sun.

Then, at last, came the day when the children of the Sun had to go away from the tribe and back to the home of their father. Before they left, they called the Incan ancestors together. They said, "Our father, the Sun, is a most beneficent Lord. He casts his light upon the earth so that the people of the earth may see to go about their daily tasks. He brings warmth where once there was cold. He nourishes the crops with his life-giving light, so that the people as well as the beasts of the land will thrive. He knows your needs, and as he passes over your villages each day, helps you to fulfill them."

As the two bid farewell to the tribe, they left this final word. "Be not unlike our father, the Sun. Be constant and regular in your daily lives. Strive not only to live in light, but to cast the light of wisdom on others that they, too, shall know the benefits of the Sun. When you meet people that live in darkness and ignorance, bring the light of worship of the Sun into their dark lives. For the Incan people are now the children of the Sun. Our father will now adopt you as his own, and you will keep his ways of goodness and knowledge among the tribes of the earth."

So it happened that the Incan people became favored by the Sun. Great temples were erected in his honor, and many daughters of the Incan people served him as Virgins of the Sun. Even the conquest of other tribes was undertaken in his name, and those they subdued were taught the ways of the Lord Sun. To this day, the Incas are still remembered as the children of the Sun.

Kuat Steals the Day

In their tribal lands in South America, the Xingu elders tell the story of how Kuat, the Sun, stole the day from the kingdom of the birds for the benefit of humanity.

In the beginning, our world knew nothing but darkness. There was no fire. There was no daylight. The only glimmer of light that gave pause to the blackness was from a few fireflies that flickered here and there. The people walked blindly about, falling, bumping into each other, searching vainly for food to sustain them. The people were slowly dying of hunger in the darkness.

Seeing the predicament of his people, the one known as Kuat, the Sun, set about to bring the day unto his land so that his people would be saved. Kuat thought and thought about how the day might be created, but could not figure a way to do it. Failing this, he thought about the kingdom of the birds. He knew well that the birds already had the day. If he could not create his own, then perhaps he could steal the day from the land of birds.

Kuat formed an image of the beast called the tapir from the root of the cassava. Within it, he placed whatever he could find that would rot and decay. In a few days, his creation was a vile, stinking mess, covered with maggots. Kuat wrapped up the maggots in a package, and summoned the flies to carry the parcel to the kingdom of the birds.

Upon their arrival in the far-off village, the flies were surrounded by birds, curious to know about the parcel they brought. The ruler of the bird kingdom, the king vulture, watched the arrival of the flies with interest. But he was a wise and cautious king, and was not ready to regard the flies' arrival without suspicion.

The king vulture ordered seats to be brought for the flies to rest on, and began to question them as to their purpose. "Why have you come here?" questioned the king. The flies replied politely, but no one could understand their words. The flies have a strange language. It seems to escape the understanding of any but the flies themselves. One by one, each of the birds passed before the flies to try to comprehend their message, and one by one, they walked away, no closer to understanding. To each of the birds, the fly language sounded like "Buzz, buzz, buzz," and nothing more.

At last, they summoned the Congo Kingbird to listen to the language of the flies. It was well known that he spoke many tongues. Perhaps he could make some sense out of this strange buzzing sound. The flies spoke slowly and deliberately, and the Congo Kingbird was able to translate their words. "Where we live, in the world below, there are many things to eat—so much that no one could possibly consume them all." The flies laid open their package, and the birds greedily downed every last bite.

"There is far more to eat where we live," said the flies. "If you like, you can come with us this very day to eat your fill." The birds made little delay in getting ready to feast in the world below.

While the flies carried out their part of the Sun's plan, Kuat was making preparations of his own. He concealed himself in the rotting image of the tapir, so that he could peek out and watch from holes where the tapir's eyes would be.

The birds arrived, and soon began to eat the insects that swarmed around the tapir. Only the hawk did not immediately come to feed. He perched at a distance and watched for some time.

With his keen eyes, the hawk discerned some movement in the eyes of the putrid tapir. Despite his precautions, the Sun had been discovered by the hawk. The other birds were given warning and took flight. In time, however, the lure of the feast brought them back, and they continued to feed on the insects that covered the rotting cassava.

After his subjects had eaten for a long time, the ruler of the birds, the great king vulture, took his own turn at the banquet. When he alit at the image, Kuat grabbed firm hold of one of his feet. Seeing that their leader had been captured by the Sun, the other birds abandoned the image and watched from a distance in safety.

"I do not wish to take your life, King Vulture," said Kuat. "I only want the day from your village. This was the purpose in bringing you here, and it is all that I would have of you. Bring me the day, and you shall fly unhindered from this world."

The Jacubim bird was ordered to return to the bird kingdom and bring back the day. Soon he returned, bedecked in the bright feathers of the macaw. As he neared, the land brightened a little with the glory of the bright feathers. But when he landed, the appearance of light dissipated. The trick had failed.

Again, he was sent to return with the day, and again, he tried to trick the Sun with a glory of feathers. Three more times, the Jacubim was sent to bring the day. Three more times he tried to trick Kuat with colorful feathers.

At last, the Guam bird was sent to retrieve the day from the bird kingdom. There were no tricks this time, and when he returned, the dark world became bright.

Kuat released the King Vulture as he had promised, and the bird king began to instruct him in the ways of the day. "In the morning, the light will be bright. In the afternoon, it will fade. Then there will be darkness, but do not think that we took it back. It will always return to you when the morning comes again."

The Sun learned that the day is for hunting, fishing, and planting. When the light fades, it is time to rest from labor, and to start anew when the light returns.

Kuat thanked the King Vulture for his help, and promised that upon the death of a large animal, he would leave its carcass for the bird to feed on. Now when the King Vulture is seen circling in the sky, we know that the Sun has kept his promise. But in light of this Xingu tale, we might regard the vulture not as a scavenger, a bird of death, but as our great benefactor—the bringer of light into a world of darkness.

Sisters of Light

In most legends, the Sun is known as a single entity—sometimes male, sometimes female, but always a lone character. Yet this is not true in every culture. The Minyong people of northern India remember two sisters who together were the origin of light.

In the beginning there was Sedi, the woman who was the earth, and Melo, the man who was the sky. In between these two giants lived the lesser creatures, the men and the animals. It happened that the two titans decided to marry.

Marriage is often a glorious occasion, but not to the creatures who dwelt between Sedi and Melo. It was feared that on their wedding day the couple would desire to come together as men and women do. When this happened, those who lived between them would certainly be crushed.

There was much discussion about how the middle creatures might save themselves from this fate. At last, it was Sedi-Dyor, largest and strongest of all, who took the matter in hand. With all of his might, he struck Melo, the giant sky man. Now perhaps the strength of Sedi-Dyor was greater than anyone could have imagined, or perhaps the great Melo was shocked by the brazen attack of the tiny man. For whatever reason, Melo fled far up into the heavens, leaving his newly wedded bride behind.

As the great Melo flew to the far reaches of heaven, Sedi gave birth to two children. The great earth woman, however, was so distraught over losing her husband that she didn't care for her newly arrived daughters. She would not nurse them, and turned away from them.

Sedi-Dyor was as great in compassion as he was in strength. He felt that since it was he that had made Melo leave his wife, it was his responsibility to find a nurse for the daughters of the Sky and the Earth. He did find a suitable nurse, and the children thrived under her loving care. As the children grew, light began to shine from them, growing brighter and brighter with each passing day.

In time, age crept up on the nurse and consumed her vitality. When death claimed this loving woman, Sedi-Dyor buried her. The daughters grieved and wept for the nurse as if she had been their own mother. Their sorrow so consumed them that they grieved themselves to death. Their light ceased to shine, and the world was in darkness once more, as it had been in the beginning of time.

The middle creatures were afraid in the darkness, and tried to think of a way to bring back the light to the world. Since the light had died with the old nurse, they thought that perhaps the secret to its return lay buried with her in her grave. The grave was dug up, and to everyone's great surprise, there were no remains of the nurse. Where the old woman had been buried only two bright shining eyes were left.

The eyes were taken to a stream to be washed. When this was done, they shone all the brighter. When the creatures peered into the shining eyes, they saw naught but their own reflection. They took the eyes to a craftsman to have him remove the images from them. When this was done, the reflections became two young girls.

One can only guess that when the daughters' light died as they pined for the old nurse, a spark of all that they were was kept alive in the loving eyes of their caretaker.

The two girls were named Bomong and Bong, and grew quickly to womanhood. They were watched closely as they grew, and not allowed to leave their house. The middle creatures feared to again suffer the loss of their beings of light.

One day Bomong, the eldest, arose from her bed. She dressed in bright clothes and shining ornaments and set out to leave the house that had become like a prison to her. As she left, her light began to shine more and more brightly. She walked far across the land, intending never to return. All that was left of her was the vision of her light peeking over the far hills.

Bong went to find her big sister. When she left the house, her light grew as her sister's had, only to a greater degree. The creatures of the middle world fainted with the heat of her light. Trees withered. Great boulders were split in two.

The people and animals of the middle world talked about the light of the two girls. They knew that the combined light of the two would bring nothing but destruction to their land, and decided to eliminate Bong, the greater of the two.

One of the creatures, the frog, waited for Bong as she walked down the path one day. As she neared, he fixed an arrow to his bow and shot the girl. Bong died immediately where she had fallen. As the life drained from her body, her light began to fade. The heat subsided. Trees came back to life. People and animals began to recover and go about their work.

When Bomong came across her sister's lifeless body, she mourned her loss—but she also feared for her own life. Perhaps, she thought, it would be decided that her own light was as offensive as her sister's, and an assassin would lie in wait for her too. Bomong sat down and placed a large rock upon her head. This stone cast a shadow over her, and darkness descended upon the world.

Men and animals were gripped by the old fear they had known in the days before when their world was plunged into darkness. They searched for the light of Bomong everywhere, but could not find it. At last, they sent the cock out to locate Bomong. After searching for a long time, the cock located the sister of light, and begged her to return her light to the world.

"No," said Bomong. "You have killed my sister. Perhaps you will take it into your heads to kill me too!" The cock swore that they would not take her life, but Bomong wanted proof. "You must first bring my sister back to life. Only then will I return to you."

The creatures of the middle world had an artisan fashion an image of the slain Bong. She was smaller that the original, but very accurate in every other detail. They put life into the image, and Bong was restored.

When Bomong heard that her sister was brought back to life, she cast down the stone from her head, and there was daylight in the world once more. A great cheer went up among the creatures of the middle world. The cock, who had been an important part of restoring light to the world, let out a proud and happy "Cock-a-doodle-do."

Now the sisters of light shine brightly through the day. Because the smaller Bong can only cast a lesser light, there is not so much heat that the world is burned up. And each dawn you can hear the evidence that these times are still remembered by the creatures of the middle world. As the first light of day appears over the hills, the cock remembers the old times as he crows his proud and happy refrain.

Owl, Dove, and Bat

There was a story told among the old Celtic tribes of how the animals came to find their place in the Sun. It begins with a journey that Owl and Dove made together, more years ago than the eldest can remember.

It was just about dusk when Owl and Dove came upon an old barn. Weary from their journey, they agreed to take refuge for the night in the barn, and set out fresh at first light. Unknown to the tired travelers, the chief of a tribe of Bats lived in the old barn with his family. Seeing the strangers enter his dwelling, and being a beast of some social grace, Bat invited Dove and Owl to share a fine dinner with himself and his family.

There was a glorious meal prepared, and Dove and Owl had their fill of a wonderful dinner and good, strong drink. When the guests had been thoroughly sated, Owl arose to speak his thanks for the hospitality of their host.

"Bat," began Owl. "Most generous is your nature. Widely is your honor known. Most highly are you respected. There is no beast on land or in the air that is of equal stature to you. You are far wiser, and much more learned than all the rest. You have more valor than the eagle. You are far more handsome than the peacock, and the sounds that you utter are more pleasing to the ear than the song of the nightingale."

Bat, as might be expected, was overcome with pride at Owl's unreserved flattery, and was quite impressed with how observant Owl was. He puffed out his chest at the recognition of his virtue, and turned to Dove to hear a refrain of his praises. Yet Dove sat in silence. She offered no praises of her own to Bat, nor did she even offer any sign of agreement with Owl's words.

All eyes turned to Dove. After a while, realizing that she was expected to speak, and not wanting to seem ungrateful for the fine meal and drink, she politely thanked her host for his hospitality. The whole Bat family scowled at Dove. They chastised her for her failure to sing the praises of Bat as the courteous Owl had done. They questioned her breeding as reflected in her lack of good manners. Dove replied quietly and honestly that she favored truth over flattery.

At this, the entire company became enraged. They beat her severely until she was hardly able to move under her own power. They turned her, wounded and bloody, out into the stormy night to suffer the harsh, cold rains.

The dawn arrived, and Dove, recovered from her injuries, flew up toward the Sun. There she met the most revered creature of the Sun, the valiant Eagle. She told Eagle how the Bats and Owl had mistreated her.

Eagle vowed that should Bats or Owls ever again fly out under the Sun, all the creatures of the air would descend upon them and treat them as they had treated Dove. He vowed also that the Doves would thenceforth be most loved by the Sun for their devotion to truth and honesty.

Never again has a flock of Owls or Bats been seen beneath the light of the Sun. They hide beneath the cover of darkness, fearful that the vow of the Sun's messenger, the Eagle, will be fulfilled.

The Legend of Scar-Face

The Algonquins tell a tale of a poor but brave hunter known as Scar-face. It was in a face-to-face confrontation with a giant grizzly bear that he earned his name. After a gallant struggle, the bear lay slain by the brave, but not before he cut an eternal reminder of the episode into the hunter's face with his claws.

The chief of Scar-face's tribe had a most desirable daughter. Like the rest of the young braves, Scar-face was enchanted by her. He longed to ask her to marry him, but knew she had already turned away many of the other braves of the tribe.

A time came when Scar-face passed by the maiden as she sat outside her lodge, her lovely face drinking in the summer Sun. He could not tear his eyes from her beauty. As it happened, one of the braves who had already been rejected by the chief's daughter also noticed his gaze. "Of what use would you be to a maid so full of grace?" said the brave. "She has already turned away the finest of our tribe. And you—of no great wealth and foul of face—you look longingly at her? I suppose you wish to wed her, as well!"

Scar-face was not enraged by the taunting of the brave. His disfigurement had invited much ridicule, and he had grown quite used to it. Instead, very quietly, very honestly, he told the brave, "That is exactly what I intend, if she will have me." It was not until these words passed his lips that Scar-face realized the depth of his love for the maiden, and knew that he would indeed ask her to marry him.

Scar-face took a few days to fortify himself enough to approach the maiden. The quest he was about to undertake was as difficult as fighting the grizzly. In time, he found the girl alone, gathering reeds by the river. He approached the chief's daughter respectfully and said, "I am a brave of no great riches, but the love for you in my heart will keep you warmer that the many pelts of wealthier braves. I am a good hunter, and can provide for you. Will you come with me to my lodge and be my wife?"

To his relief, the maid looked right through his disfigurement to his great love. "I have no need of riches, for my father is chief, and abundantly wealthy. Yet I cannot marry you, for it has been decreed by the Sun God that I may never wed. It is only he that can release me."

Scar-face was saddened, and saw little hope that the Sun God would free the maiden. Still, he promised her that he would seek out the Sun God and try to gain his blessing on their union. As a sign, so that the maiden would know for certain that she had been released, the Sun God would be asked to remove the scars from the brave's face.

For many seasons, Scar-face sought the home of the Sun God. He asked the creatures of the wood which direction would carry him to his destination. He questioned the birds, the bear, and the badger, but none could help direct him in his journey. At last, he met a wolverine who said that he had been to the dwelling of the Sun God, and could direct the brave along his path.

Following the instructions of the wolverine, Scar-face traveled far and long until he came to the edge of a great water. The water was too broad to cross, and Scar-face sat sadly on the banks, pondering his predicament. After a while, two swans came by and told the brave to climb upon their backs. The swans brought Scar-face safely to the other side of the water.

There he was met by Apisirahts, the Morning Star. "It is my father you seek," he said. "Follow me to the lodge of the Sun God." When they arrived, they were welcomed by the Moon Goddess Kokomikis, wife of the Sun God. In a short time, the Sun God himself appeared, brilliant in all his shining glory. He greeted Scar-face cordially and invited him to stay for a while as a guest within his abode, and a hunting companion for his son.

Grateful for the kind reception, and fearful of speaking his purpose too quickly, Scar-face accepted the offer of hospitality. "Be warned, however," said the Sun God, "to stay away from the Great Water, for there are birds of prey that dwell at the water's edge. They seek to ravage my son, the Morning Star."

One day as they headed out for the hunt as usual, Apisirahts raced ahead of Scar-face. Ignoring the danger, he had gotten it into his head to bring down the savage birds of which his father had spoken. As he neared the Great Water, Scar-face closed the gap between them. Just as the monstrous birds were about to swoop down on Morning Star with their mighty claws, Scar-face let his arrow fly. It struck true, and saved the Morning Star from certain death.

The Sun God was grateful to the brave for saving the life of his son. Willing to grant any request that Scar-face would name, he consented to release the chief's daughter to be wed. As a sign, he removed the disfigurement from the face of the brave, and restored him to his original beauty. "Go now," said the Sun God, "return to your own village, and wed the maiden that makes your heart swell with love."

When Scar-face returned to his tribe, the maiden could scarcely recognize him. When she did, she knew that the vanishing of the marks that had marred his face meant that he had been successful in his meeting with the Sun God.

The two were wed that very day. To the honor of the Sun, they raised a medicine lodge. The brave hunter became known as Smooth-face from that day forward.

The Incestuous Light

In Greenland there is a folk tale about the very beginning of time, when the world was in darkness. The creation had produced the earth, and the people who inhabit the lands. The miracle of fire had been given to men and women. But except for the pale light from their torches and lamps, the first people lived their lives in darkness.

To pass the time, men and women played games in the darkness. Some of them were innocent, childlike games. And why not? After all, these were the children of the earth. The were newly created, and just learning the ways of life. As they began to discover more about the world around them and about themselves, the nature of their play seemed to change.

Just barely passing puberty, they began to experiment with the pleasures of the body, and they began to discover each other. As if in a primitive game of Spin the Bottle, all the men and women would gather inside their dwelling. There in the dark, they would find a partner, and enjoy each other as completely as their desires would carry them. When the game was done, each couple would emerge from the dwelling, light a fire, and by the light of the flame discover with whom they had played in the darkness. Often did they pursue the pleasures of the darkness, and when they first saw the face of their partner in the fire-light, they were often amused to see who their secret partner turned out to be.

One day, the children of the earth lands were pursuing this favorite pastime. As always, the couples enjoyed each other fully, and emerged to discover the identity of their secret lover. Moon Man, as he had so many times before, strolled hand in hand from the darkness of the dwelling into the illumination of the fire. When he looked upon the face of his partner, he was astonished and shocked to see his sister, Sun Woman, looking back at him.

Sun Woman was even more disturbed by the situation than her brother. In disgust and horror that she had lain down with her own brother, Sun Woman tore her breasts from her body, and threw them down before her brother. Then, with torch in hand, she flew into the sky, trying to outrun her shame and embarrassment. Moon Man, concerned for the well-being of his sister, took a torch in hand and followed her. As he chased Sun Woman, the flame in Moon Man's torch went out, leaving only a glowing cinder.

To this day, Moon Man and Sun Woman continue their eternal chase across the sky. Sun Woman leads the way with her brightly burning torch. Moon Man forever pursues her with his less brilliant light.

Coyote's Bright Adventure

Throughout the world there are cultures that agree that the universe was begun in darkness, though stories differ as to how the first illumination pierced that early, dark world. There are many different gods, goddesses, heroes and beasts credited with bringing the first light. Among the Cahto tribe of California, the legend is told of Coyote, and how it was he who was responsible for lifting the world from darkness.

Coyote was taking a nap. He was having some trouble finding a comfortable position in which to take his rest. At first, he lay down with his head in the north. Unable to find the comfort he sought, he changed position and placed his head to the south. This didn't seem to work well either, so he lay his head down in the west. Finally, he tried the east. This seemed to be the best so far, and Coyote drifted off into a pleasant nap.

While sleeping peacefully, Coyote's forehead began to feel uncomfortably hot. It was so uncomfortable, in fact, that he was taken from his slumber. When he was fully awake, he realized that the feeling that had roused him from sleep was the product of his own dreams. He had been dreaming about the Sun. It was this dream that gave Coyote the idea to go and get the Sun, and bring it back as a gift for the people of the earth.

Now, at this time, the Sun was kept by an old woman in her house. Coyote knew that he must journey to the place where the Sun was held captive, and, very probably, have to trick the old woman to gain the Sun's release. Resolute in the success of his mission, Coyote set out on his journey to the house of the Sun's confinement.

Along the way, Coyote encountered three creatures. These he recognized as dogs. However, in a world of darkness, it is not easy to guess the identity of those you meet. In reality, Coyote's companions were field mice. Still, his new companions agreed to help in the liberation of the Sun. It would be their job to bite through the bindings that hold the Sun. Coyote would then be free to make off with the prize.

When the troop of liberators arrived at the old woman's house, Coyote knocked on the door. "I'm sorry to trouble you, old woman," said Coyote. "I wish little from you. My journey has been long. I wish no food or drink, but just a quiet little corner where I can lie down and rest from my weary travels." The old woman agreed to Coyote's request. She offered him a corner of her house in which to lie down, and a blanket to keep him warm.

This is when the plan begins to be put into action. Coyote settled down in his appointed corner and draped the blanket over himself as if preparing to sleep. "Forgive me, old woman. Sometimes I don't easily find my way to slumber. It helps if I can sing myself to sleep. With your kind permission, I will sing my song quietly, and soon be so silent that you do not even know I'm here."

The old woman agreed to this request, and Coyote began to sing a lullaby. The sweet song, however, was not truly for the benefit of Coyote, but for the old woman. It worked better than expected. Soon the old woman was deep in slumber, and Coyote's scheme could be carried out.

Without delay, Coyote summoned his companions to begin their work of biting through the straps that bind the Sun. Now had his new friends truly been dogs as he had thought, the job would have been quickly completed. One snap of their sharp teeth would have severed the Sun's bonds. However, mice cannot accomplish the appointed task quite as swiftly. Nevertheless, the three small creatures determinedly began the work of gnawing through the Sun's bindings.

By the time the mice had finished severing the straps that held the Sun, the woman was not as deeply asleep as she had been. Coyote knew that he had to move quickly to carry off the Sun. As swiftly as he could, Coyote raced off, pulling the Sun behind him. However, he was not unseen as he left the old woman's house.

Mole saw Coyote and called out, "A thief is stealing the Sun!" Fortunately, the Mole is a creature of little voice. His alarm was not loud enough to rouse the old woman from her light slumber. Lizard also saw Coyote making off with the Sun. Coyote felt fortunate, for Lizard is a creature with no voice at all, so he could not alert the old woman. But in a surprise gesture, Lizard picked up a stick and began beating the old woman's house. The racket awakened the old woman, and she saw what Coyote was doing.

The old woman sprang up and gave chase to Coyote. "Why are you carrying off the Sun?" she called after him. "It is sorely in need of repair, and I'm not finished fixing it." Her words gave Coyote pause until he realized that this crafty old woman was trying to trick him. But this clever ploy, though unsuccessful, had slowed Coyote in his pace, and the old woman was closing the gap between them. "You are not fixing the Sun," retorted Coyote. "In fact, you are hiding it!" As she continued to gain on him, Coyote called back, "Sly woman, you are almost upon me. Stop where you are and turn to stone!" These words had scarcely left Coyote's mouth when the old woman began to harden, stopped in her tracks by Coyote's magic.

Coyote continued his journey without his pursuer. When he arrived home, he took out his hunting knife. From the Sun he carved a Moon and stars, which he released to the night. The largest piece that was left became the Sun we know today.

Grateful for his gift of light, the people honored Coyote with many presents. Even today, Coyote takes a special place in the hearts of the people, and is remembered with glory in the legends they tell.

Rabbit Snares the Sun

*L*ong ago, there lived a Rabbit whose adventures are still remembered and recounted by the storytellers of the Lakota nation. Here is the story of how he snared the Sun.

Every morning, Rabbit arose early. He left his old grandmother, who dwelt with him, asleep in the lodge while he set out for the day's hunting. But no matter how early Rabbit set out, when he reached the hunting ground there was evidence of another hunter who arrived at the hunt earlier that he did. In the earth were tracks of the early riser. He bent down to examine the prints. They were made by someone with a very long foot.

Rabbit resolved to rise even earlier the next day to beat this other hunter to the hunting ground. When he arrived, however, it was exactly as it had been on every other morning. The trail of the long-footed hunter was already marked in the earth. And just as on the previous days, there was no sign of the stranger himself, only his familiar footprint.

This infuriated the Rabbit. When he returned to the lodge, he spoke with his grandmother about the problem. "Grandmother," spoke the Rabbit, "each day when I set out to the hunting ground, I find that another has been there before me. I faithfully set my traps, but the one who first arrives has already caught the best game and frightened the rest away."

Grandmother listened quietly to Rabbit, nodding with tender understanding. Finally, Rabbit said, "I will set a trap for Long Foot, and put an end to his early hunt!" "Why," asked Grandmother, "has this other hunter not the right to hunt as you do? Has this stranger whom you have never seen done you harm in some way?"

"It doesn't matter!" said Rabbit. "It is enough that I despise this Long Foot." With that, Rabbit stalked off and headed to the hunting ground. There, he hid himself among the bushes until nightfall. Under cover of darkness, Rabbit worked quickly to enact his plan. With a strong bowstring, he assembled a snare and laid it in the place where the long footprints were usually found. Having completed his task, he headed home to his lodge.

The next morning, he went out earlier than usual to the hunting ground. He was anxious to examine the trap he had set for the unsuspecting stranger. When he arrived at his snare, he was elated to find that he had, indeed, caught the stranger. He was so excited about his success that he did not even stop long enough to notice who he had entrapped. As fast as he could run, he went straight home to share his glory with Grandmother. When she heard the news, Grandmother asked the Rabbit who the mysterious hunter had turned out to be. When his excitement subsided a bit, he realized that he had never stopped to notice.

Embarrassed about his oversight, and curious to discover the identity of Long Foot, Rabbit returned to the woods to look at his prize. When he arrived at the site of the trap, he saw that it was the bright Sun caught in his snare. The Sun had become more than a little enraged over his unfortunate circumstances. "How dare you have the audacity to lay a trap for the Sun! Come and loose these bonds at once!"

The Rabbit approached the Sun very cautiously. He did not wish to invoke the vengeance of the Sun. As quickly as he could, Rabbit slit the snare with his knife, releasing his angry prisoner. The Sun flew swiftly into the sky and was soon out of sight.

Now, if you look closely, you'll see that the fur between Rabbit's shoulders is yellow. This is where he was scorched by the hot Sun when he cut the snare to release him.

Red Riding Sun

It is said that the ageless tale of Little Red Riding Hood first originated as a Sun story. A hint of the truth of this is the prominent garment of red, the color of fire, the fire of the Sun.

As Red Riding Hood begins her journey, she is a vision of youth. She is the first light of the Sun, the dawn's first light. Just as her counterpart travels across the sky, Red Riding Hood begins the long journey through the wood.

She travels to her grandmother, a vision of old age, just as the Sun makes a path toward the final hours of the day at sunset. But when she arrives, the wolf, who represents the darkness, has already devoured the grandmother, and awaits the arrival of Red Riding Hood, who seems destined to suffer the same fate as the old woman.

Had it not been for the benevolent woodcutter, Little Red Riding Hood would have been consumed by the wolf, and darkness would emerge victorious over light. But in the nick of time, the woodcutter bursts into the house and chases away the forces of darkness. The solar Little Red Riding Hood is free to dawn another day. The dark wolf is kept apart from the light by the "divine intervention" of the woodcutter.

Now, in this version of the tale, we are not rid of the darkness, but it is kept away from the Sun, and never gets close enough to devour it. So when the Sun is overhead, we know that the darkness will not prevail. And at nightfall, when the wolf is visible, we need not fear for the safety of the Sun. We know that Little Red Riding Hood is at a safe distance from the darkness under the protection of the woodcutter.

Maui's Sun Net

The people of Manihiki tell the legends of the god-hero Maui, who was responsible for a great many gifts to the people. He brought fire for warmth and for cooking. He pulled up islands from the depths of the sea to create dry land on which the people could live.

In Maui's time, the Sun raced along its course, scarcely slowing long enough to separate the day from the night. This seemed a less than ideal situation to Maui, and he decided to take some action to alter the swift pace of the Sun's journey.

Out of ropes he fashioned by hand, Maui constructed a great strong net, strong enough to capture the Sun as it raced across the sky. Were it only the size and weight of the Sun to be considered, perhaps the net that Maui had made would have served its purpose. However, he did not take the intense heat of the blazing Sun into account. When Maui managed to catch the Sun in his net, the ropes were burned by the Sun's fire, and he easily escaped his would-be captor.

Maui sat down to repair his net and attempt to trap his prey once again. Two, three, four times he tried. Each time, his net was burned and he had to begin repairs anew. Each time, the Sun continued on his speedy travels, unhindered by Maui's efforts.

At last, Maui gave up on trying to catch the Sun in his net. He made a lariat of his sister's hair. When the Sun emerged from the hole in the sky that leads from the world of its home, Maui snared it in his lariat and held it tightly. Once he had his captive's attention, Maui entreated the Sun to slow down in his journey. When the Sun agreed, Maui let him go on. But just to be certain that the Sun continued to fulfill its promise, Maui left the ropes hanging from the Sun. Should the vow be broken, Maui can grasp the hanging ropes and imprison the Sun once again.

The ropes that still hang from the Sun are most visible in the morning hours and at the time of its setting. They appear as rays of sunlight extending down from the bright Sun and reaching toward the earth. If ever there is a need, it is said that Maui will take up the ropes again to remind the Sun of its ancient promise.

Ictinike and the Buzzard

*I*n the legendry of some cultures, the Sun is a lofty, unapproachable being. However, often there are children of the Sun who take on a more human aspect. Among the Kiowa tribes, such a legend recounts the story of Ictinike, the fallen son of the Sun God. Because he is no longer in the good graces of the Sun, we can tell of his adventures without fear of reprisal from his father.

Ictinike had somehow lost favor with his father, the Sun, and was thrown out of his father's lodge in the heavens. It is said that all the evil known to humanity was taught to them by Ictinike. It was Ictinike who taught the tribes the ways of war. It is he that is ultimately responsible for the death of every warrior who fell in a raid. He is well-known for his deceitful manner, his fine command of trickery, and his mastery of lies.

The beasts of the earth also know well the reputation of Ictinike. All living creatures dislike, distrust, and fear this son of the Sun God. Perhaps it was this hatred of Ictinike that led to the actions of Buzzard, as told in the Kiowa legend.

After a difficult day of travel, Ictinike came upon Buzzard perched on the stout limb of a tree. Tired and sore, the son of the Sun asked Buzzard to help him along his way. He asked to climb upon the bird's back to continue his journey and give his swollen feet a rest. With little hesitation, Buzzard consented to Ictinike's request.

Seating the son of the Sun God on his back, Buzzard beat his strong wings against the air and soared high into the sky. Ictinike was grateful for Buzzard's help, and sped along on his journey with the aid of his benefactor. After a time, the pair flew above a hollow tree. When they did, Buzzard stopped his forward flight and began to circle round and round the tree below.

Ictinike became uneasy with Buzzard's strange behavior. He asked why he had stopped to hover above this hollow tree, and asked him to continue along the way. Buzzard said nothing, but swooped down from the sky and dived toward the tree. As he neared the tree, Buzzard quickly turned, throwing his passenger forcefully in the direction of it. When Ictinike regained his senses after the fall, he found that the trickery of Buzzard had made him a prisoner within the tree's hollow.

For a long time, Ictinike lay trapped in his wooden prison, unable to extricate himself from his situation. At last, a hunting party made camp near the tree. Ictinike took this opportunity to gain his freedom. Certainly, with his foul reputation, no one would willingly help him out of his circumstances, so he resorted to his gift for deceit to gain his release.

As it happened, Ictinike was wearing the skins of raccoons that day. He stuck the tails of the skins out of some cracks in the trunk of the tree and began to wave them about. Three women from the hunting party saw the raccoon tails signalling from the hollow tree. They assumed that a number of raccoons must be trapped within the trunk, and began to make a hole in the tree and capture the helpless animals.

The women worked quickly to claim their prize. As soon as the hole was large enough, Ictinike sprang from the tree. His liberators fled at the sight of him. It was then that his thoughts turned toward revenge against Buzzard, who had landed him in this predicament in the first place.

Ictinike lay down on the ground, quite motionless, pretending to be dead. When the birds of prey saw his apparently lifeless body covered in raccoon skin, they swiftly came from the sky to feast on this fortunate find. It was Eagle, Hawk, and Rook who first arrived at the scene. They began pecking hungrily at the motionless body of Ictinike. Still, he did not stir.

By and by, Buzzard came flying overhead. He saw the company feasting below, and did not delay in joining them at their meal. But as Buzzard landed on the motionless body of Ictinike, the son of the Sun God moved quickly. He tore the feathers from the head of Buzzard in repayment for his trickery. This is why Buzzard, to this day, has no feathers on the top of his head.

Epilogue

Tales of simplicity, tales of glory, tales of death, of life, of compassion and devastation—there is little that has not been perceived as being within the reaches of the Sun. From the farthest reaches of time, when getting through each new day was an end in itself, the Sun watched from overhead.

No sadness, no joy, no honor, no shame has ever arisen among the peoples of the earth outside the sight of the eye of the Sun. There has been no birth, no death that the divine star of the day has not witnessed. Even the thief in the night is reminded by the silver reflection of the Sun's brilliant light in the face of the Moon that there can be no act that is not under the scrutiny of the all-seeing father or the all-knowing mother.

If there is nothing more to be gained from the legends of the world, let us learn that as the luminaries in the heavens have been perceived as male or female, as father or mother of creation, so are those who dwell beneath their splendor made of male and female natures.

The Sun, often the personification of the masculine principle of the universe, can never cast its light upon the day but for the Moon, the feminine orb. So is it that man and woman, each in their own right, are but a shadow of the glory that their union becomes. In all their separate manifestations the male and female principles of the universe may express the height of emotion, the depth of love, the epitome of adventure. Yet, it is only in their combination that they can know creation.

The Sun brings forth the light,
the Moon holds it in darkness.
As above, so below.

Appendix A:
The Solar Gods

Agni (Hindu)
Ahura Mazda (Persian)
Amun (Egyptian)
Anansi (African)
Anu (Babylonian)
Apollo (Greek)
Apu Panchau (Incan)
Aton (Egyptian)
Atum (Egyptian)
Baldur (Norse)
Bel (Babylonian)
Dagda (Celtic)
Dahzbog (Slavic)
Dumuzi (Sumerian)
El (Hebrew)
Freyr (Norse)
Helios (Greek)
Horus (Egyptian)
Huitzilopochtli (Aztec)
Indra (Hindu)
Inti (Incan)

Janus (Roman)
Khepera (Egyptian)
Llew Llaw Gyffes (Welsh)
Lucifer (Judeo-Christian)
Lugh (Irish)
Manco Capac (Incan)
Marduk (Sumerian)
Merodach (Babylonian)
Mithras (Persian)
Odhinn (Norse)
Osiris (Egyptian)
Ra (Egyptian)
Shakura (Pawnee)
Shamash (Babylonian)
Sin (Haidan)
Surya (Hindu)
Svarog (Slavic)
Svintovit (Slavic)
Varuna (Hindu)
Vishnu (Hindu)
Vulcan (Roman)

Appendix B:
The Solar Goddesses

Amaterasu (Japanese)
Ba'alat (Phoenician)
Bast (Egyptian)
Gauri (Indian)
Hae-Sun (Korean)
Hathor (Egyptian)
Hsi Wang Mu (Chinese)
Saule (Baltic)
Sakhmet (Egyptian)

Sequineq (Eskimo)
Sulis (British)
Tso (Yucchi)
Unelanuhi (Cherokee)
Ushas (Hindu)
Vesta (Roman)
Walu (Aborigine)
Yhi (Aborigine)

Selected Bibliography

Hamilton, Virginia. *In The Beginning*. Orlando, FL: Harcourt Brace Jovanovich, 1988.

Gordon, Stewart. *The Encyclopedia of Myths and Legends*. London: Headline Book Publishing, 1993.

James, T. G. H. *Myths and Legends of Ancient Egypt*. Toronto: Bantam Books, 1972.

Karas, Sheryl Ann. *The Solstice Evergreen*. Boulder Creek, CA: Aslan Publishing, 1958.

Krupp, Dr. E. C. *Beyond the Blue Horizon*. New York: HarperCollins Publishers, 1991.

Leland, Charles G. *Aradia: Gospel of the Witches*. New York: Samuel Weiser, 1974.

Matthews, John. *A Celtic Reader*. London: The Aquarian Press, 1991.

MacKenzie, Donald A. *China and Japan*. London: Senate/Studio Editions Ltd., 1994.

MacKenzie, Donald A. *India*. London: Senate/Studio Editions Ltd., 1994.

Monaghan, Patricia. *O Mother Sun!* Freedom, CA: The Crossing Press, 1994.

Nividita, Sister and Coomaraswamy, Ananda K. *Hindus and Buddhists*. London: Senate/Studio Editions, 1994.

Sharpe, J. Edward and Underwood, Thomas B. *American Indian Cooking & Herb Lore*. Cherokee, NC: Cherokee Publications, 1973.

Spence, Lewis. *Introduction to Mythology*. London: Senate/Studio Editions, 1994.

———. *Myths of the North American Indians*. New York: Gramercy Books, 1994.

———. *Mexico and Peru*. London: Studio Editions Ltd., 1994

Squire, Charles. *Celtic Myth and Legend*. Van Nuys, CA: Newcastle Publishing Co., 1975.

VanOver, Raymond. *Sun Songs: Creation Myths from Around the World*. New York: New American Library/Mentor, 1980.

Stay in Touch...

Llewellyn publishes hundreds of books on your favorite subjects.

On the following pages you will find listed some books now available on related subjects. Your local bookstore stocks most of these and will stock new Llewellyn titles as they become available. We value your patronage.

Order by Phone

Call toll-free within the U.S. and Canada, 1–800–THE MOON.
In Minnesota call (612) 291–1970.
We accept Visa, MasterCard, and American Express.

Order by Mail

Send the full price of your order (MN residents add 7% sales tax) in U.S. funds to:

> Llewellyn Worldwide
> P.O. Box 64383, Dept. K343-3
> St. Paul, MN 55164–0383, U.S.A.

Postage and Handling

- • $4.00 for orders $15.00 and under
- • $5.00 for orders over $15.00
- • No charge for orders over $100.00 to U.S., Canada, and Mexico

We ship UPS in the continental United States. Orders shipped to P.O. boxes and to Alaska, Hawaii, and Puerto Rico will be sent first-class mail. Orders to Canada and Mexico will ship via surface mail.

International orders: Airmail—add freight equal to price of each book to the total price of order, plus $5.00 for each non-book item (audiotapes, etc.); surface mail—add $1.00 per item.

Allow 4–6 weeks delivery on all orders. Postage and handling rates subject to change.

Group Discounts

We offer a 20% quantity discount to group leaders or agents. You must order a minimum of 5 copies of the same book to get our special quantity price.

Prices subject to change without notice.

Free Catalog

Get a free copy of our color catalog, *New Worlds of Mind and Spirit*. Subscribe for just $10.00 in the United States and Canada ($30.00 overseas, air mail). Many bookstores carry *New Worlds*—ask for it!

Moon Lore:
Myths & Folklore from Around the World
Gwydion O'Hara

Most of us love stories. But the rich messages spun in folklore—especially in oral traditions—are not found in the media from which we get most of our knowledge today. Fairy tales rehashed in media mega-productions don't often serve the true function of a fairy or folk tale. Where are the stories that entertain, enlighten, and bring us closer together?

Moon Lore is a collection of tales about the people of many lands and times. The common thread connecting the stories is the Moon: the heavenly body that has guided us since the beginning of time. Today, Moon mythology continues to bind the people of the world together, reflecting our diverse lives in all her faces. *Moon Lore*'s magical characters and settings spring to life in tales of jealousy, fear, triumph, celebration, love, and challenge. Find out what the Hindi Wise men see in the Moon (it's not a man's face). Jack and Jill are in *Moon Lore*, but in this Germanic variation, magic brew is what they fetch, and they never tumble down the hill! Chapters are divided into 13 segments, each lunar month presenting a new myth from Celtic, Chinese, Native American, and other traditions and cultures.

1-56718-342-5
5.25 x 8, 256 pp., index, softcover $12.95

To order, call 1-800-THE MOON
Prices subject to change without notice

Lord of Light & Shadow:
The Many Faces of the God
D. J. Conway

Early humans revered the great Goddess and all Her personalized aspects,
but they also revered the God as Her
necessary and important consort/lover/son. *Lord of Light
and Shadow* leads you through the myths of the world's diverse cultures to find the archetypal Pagan God hidden behind all of them. He is a being with the traits and aspects
that women secretly desire in men, and that men desire to
emulate. The patriarchal religions assimilated the ancient
spirit of the Pagan God—in one form or another—into
their scriptures. Yet, despite the deliberate changes to his
identity, there is something about the God that could never be destroyed. By searching for the original Pagan God in
these mythologies, you will find his spiritual essence and
the path to the truth.

1-56178-177-5
240 pp., 6 x 9, illus., softcover $14.95

To order, call 1-800-THE MOON
Prices subject to change without notice

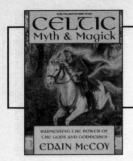

Celtic Myth & Magick:
Harnessing the Power of the
Gods and Goddesses
Edain McCoy

Tap into the mythic power of the Celtic goddesses, gods, heroes and heroines to aid your spiritual quests and magickal goals. *Celtic Myth & Magick* explains how to use creative ritual and pathworking to align yourself with the energy of these archetypes, whose potent images live deep within your psyche.

Celtic Myth & Magick begins with an overview of 49 different types of Celtic Paganism followed today, then gives specific instructions for evoking and invoking the energy of the Celtic pantheon. Three detailed pathworking texts will take you on an inner journey where you'll join forces with the archetypal images of Cuchulain, Queen Maeve and Merlin the Magician to bring their energies directly into your life. The last half of the book clearly details the energies of over 300 Celtic deities and mythic figures so you can evoke or invoke the appropriate deity to attain a specific goal.

This inspiring, well-researched book will help solitary Pagans who seek to expand the boundaries of their practice to form working partnerships with the divine.

1–56718–661–0
7 x 10, 464 pp., softcover $19.95

Glamoury:
Magic of the Celtic Green World
Steve Blamires

Glamoury refers to an Irish Celtic magical tradition that is truly holistic, satisfying the needs of the practitioner on the physical, mental, and spiritual levels. This guidebook offers practical exercises and modern versions of time-honored philosophies that will expand your potential into areas previously closed to you.

We have moved so far away from our ancestors' closeness to the Earth—the Green World—that we have nearly forgotten some very important truths about human nature. *Glamoury* brings these truths to light so you can take your rightful place in the Green World. Experience the world in a more balanced, meaningful way. Meet helpers and guides from the Otherworld who will become your valued friends. Live in tune with the seasons and gauge your inner growth in relation to the Green World around you.

The ancient Celts couched their wisdom in stories and legends. Today, intuitive people can learn much from these tales. *Glamoury* presents a system based on Irish Celtic mythology to guide you back to the harmony with life's cycles that our ancestors knew.

1-56718-069-8
6 x 9, 352 pp., illus., softcover $16.95

The Grail Castle:
Male Myths & Mysteries in the
Celtic Tradition
Kenneth Johnson &
Marguerite Elsbeth

Explore the mysteries that lie at the core of being male when you take a quest into the most powerful myth of Western civilization: the Celtic-Teutonic-Christian myth of the Grail Castle.

The Pagan Celtic culture's world view—which stressed an intense involvement with the magical world of nature—strongly resonates for men today because it offers a direct experience with the spirit often lacking in their lives. This book describes the four primary male archetypes—the King or Father, the Hero or Warrior, the Magician or Wise Man, and the Lover—which the authors exemplify with stories from the Welsh *Mabinogion*, the Ulster Cycle, and other old Pagan sources. Exercises and meditations designed to activate these inner myths will awaken men to how myths—as they live on today in the collective unconscious and popular culture— shape their lives. Finally, men will learn how to heal the Fisher King—who lies at the heart of the Grail Castle myth—to achieve integration of the four archetypal paths.

1-56718-369-7
224 pp., 6 x 9, illus., index $14.95

To order, call 1-800-THE MOON
Prices subject to change without notice

Isle of Avalon: Sacred Mysteries of Arthur & Glastonbury Tor
Nicholas R. Mann

Journey to a land where groves of ancient trees echo with the baying of hounds on a Wild Hunt ... where mysterious revolving castles, red dragons, and bubbling cauldrons are intrinsic features of the landscape. This land is the Isle of Avalon—the magickal entrance to the ancient Underworld of the Celts. This fascinating book fully describes all aspects of this powerful sacred site's incredible landscape, history, and mythology.

The ancient Celts, and the people before them, built an entire doctrine of death and rebirth around this mystical place. *Isle of Avalon* was written to restore the sense of the magical realm of the Otherworld to Western consciousness. It fully describes the physical and sacred topography of the British Isle of Avalon (pictured in beautiful photos) as well as its symbols, architecture, history, and accounts of visitation. *Isle of Avalon* also examines the magickal and spiritual implications of Avalon as an actual entrance to the Underworld.

Journey to this magical place whose landscape resonates with the human heart, mind, and body to create a gateway to another dimension—and open a doorway to the eternal.

1-56718-459-6
6 x 9, 240 pp., illus., softcover $14.95

The 21 Lessons of Merlyn: A Study in Druid Magic & Lore
Douglas Monroe

For those with an inner drive to touch genuine Druidism—or who feel that the lore of King Arthur touches them personally—*The 21 Lessons of Merlyn* will come as an engrossing adventure and psychological journey into history and magic. This is a complete introductory course in Celtic Druidism, packaged within the framework of 21 authentic and expanded folk story/lessons that read like a novel.

These lessons, set in late Celtic Britain ca. A.D. 500, depict the training and initiation of the real King Arthur at the hands of the real Merlyn-the-Druid: one of the last great champions of Paganism within the dawning age of Christianity. As you follow the boy Arthur's apprenticeship from his first encounter with Merlyn in the woods, you can study your own program of Druid apprenticeship with the detailed practical ritual applications that follow each story. The 21 folk tales were collected by the author in Britain and Wales during a ten-year period; the Druidic teachings are based on the actual, never-before-published 16th-century manuscript titled *The Book of Pheryllt*.

0-87542-496-1
420 pp., 6 x 9, illus., photos, softcover $12.95

Magickal, Mythical, Mystical Beasts: How to Invite Them into Your Life
D. J. Conway

Unicorns ... centaurs ... bogies and brownies. Here is a "Who's Who" of mystical creatures, an introduction to them, their history, and how they can be co-magicians in magickal workings. Ride Pegasus on a soul journey to the Moon. Call on the Phoenix for strength and renewing energy when facing trials in life. In ancient times, magicians knew the esoteric meanings of these beings and called on them for aid. This ability remains within us today, latent in our superconscious minds, waiting for us to re-establish communication with our astral helpers. Short chapters on candle burning, ritual, and amulets and talismans help you more easily and safely work with these creatures.

1-56718-176-7
272 pp., 6 x 9, 80 illus., softcover $14.95

His Story: Masculinity in the Post-Patriarchal World
Nicholas R. Mann

His Story was written for men of European descent who are seeking a new definition of being. The patriarchal world view dominating Western thought has cut men off from the traditions that once directly connected them to the nature of their masculinity. This book offers them a means to locate and connect with their birthright—the "native tradition" that lives in the deepest core of their being—by drawing on the pre-Christian era's conception of a man's true masculine nature.

His Story contrasts patriarchal and pre-patriarchal ideas about masculine identity, self-definition, sexuality, symbology, and spirituality—then provides a wealth of information on traditions and mythology that encompass many masculine archetypes, from those of the Grail legends to the Green Man, the Wild Man and the Horned God. Finally, the book reveals how men can connect again with these traditions and their own inherent source of personal power, thus transforming their relationships to those around them and to the world.

1-56718-458-8
336 pp., 6 x 9, softcover $16.95

To order, call 1-800-THE MOON
Prices subject to change without notice

The Mysteries of Isis: Her Worship and Magick
deTraci Regula

For 6,000 years, Isis has been worshiped as a powerful yet benevolent goddess who loves and cares for those who call on Her. Here, for the first time, Her secrets and mysteries are revealed in an easy-to-understand form so you can bring the power of this great and glorious goddess into your life.

The Mysteries of Isis is filled with practical information on the modern practice of Isis' worship. Other books about Isis treat Her as an entirely Egyptian goddess, but this book reveals that she is a universal goddess with many faces, who has been present in all places and in all times. Simple yet effective rituals and exercises will show you how to forge your unique personal alliance with Isis: prepare for initiation into Her four key mysteries, divine the future using the Sacred Scarabs, perform purification and healing rites, celebrate Her holy days, travel to your own inner temple, cast love spells, create your own tools and amulets, and much more. Take Isis as your personal goddess and your worship and connection with the divine will be immeasurably enriched.

1-56178-560-6
320 pp., 7 x 10, illus., softcover $19.95

To order, call 1-800-THE MOON
Prices subject to change without notice

**Entering the Summerland:
Customs and Rituals of
Transition into the Afterlife**
Edain McCoy

All of us must face it sooner or later—the devastating loss of a loved one. For Pagans, the period of mourning can be especially trying, simply because many are isolated from a community that shares their spiritual viewpoint of death and the afterlife. Unlike the mainstream religions, paganism has had no written guide specifically designed to offer comfort and direction to the bereaved—until now.

Entering the Summerland fills this need by providing rituals for healing and passing, as well as practical ideas about dealing with grief. *Entering the Summerland* builds concepts and ideas about death into a framework for open discussion, ritual structure, funeral planning, and bereavement support. It also attempts to legitimize griefs that are not yet acceptable to the larger society in which we live, such as mourning the loss of a pet or a familiar.

1-56718-665-3
256 pp., 7 x 10, illus., softcover $17.95